*FROUDACITY.*

" Blown by surmises, jealousies, conjectures."

" Why dost thou show to the apt thoughts of men the things that ARE NOT ?"—SHAKESPEARE.

# FROUDACITY

*WEST INDIAN FABLES BY JAMES
ANTHONY FROUDE*

EXPLAINED BY

## J. J. THOMAS

AUTHOR OF

" *The Creole Grammar* "

PHILADELPHIA

GEBBIE AND COMPANY

1890

# PREFACE.

LAST year had well advanced towards its middle—in fact it was already April, 1888—before Mr. Froude's book of travels in the West Indies became known and generally accessible to readers in those Colonies.

My perusal of it in Grenada about the period above mentioned disclosed, thinly draped with rhetorical flowers, the dark outlines of a scheme to thwart political aspiration in the Antilles. That project is sought to be realized by deterring the home authorities from granting an elective local legislature, however restricted in character, to any of the Colonies not yet enjoying such an advantage. An argument based on the composition of the inhabitants of those Colonies is confidently relied upon to confirm the inexorable mood of Downing Street.

Over-large and ever-increasing,—so runs the argument,—the African element in the population of the West Indies is, from its past history and its actual tendencies, a standing menace to the continuance of civilization and religion. An immediate catastrophe, social, political, and moral, would most assuredly be brought about by the granting of full elective rights to dependencies thus inhabited. Enlightened statesmanship should at once perceive the immense benefit that would ultimately result from such refusal of the franchise. The cardinal recommendation of that refusal is that it would avert definitively the political domination of the Blacks, which must inevitably be the outcome of any concession of the modicum of right so earnestly desired. The exclusion of the Negro vote being inexpedient, if not impossible, the exercise of electoral powers by the Blacks must lead to their returning candidates of their own race to the local legislatures, and that, too, in numbers preponderating according to the majority of the Negro electors. The Negro legislators thus supreme in the councils of the Colonies would straightway proceed to pass vindictive and retaliatory laws against their white fellow-colonists. For it is only fifty years since the White man and the Black man stood in the reciprocal relations of master and slave. Whilst those relations subsisted, the white masters inflicted, and the black slaves had to endure, the hideous atrocities that are inseparable from the system of slavery. Since Emancipation, the enormous strides made in self-advancement by the ex-slaves have only had the effect of provoking a resentful uneasiness in the bosoms of the ex-masters. The former bondsmen, on their side, and like their brethren of Hayti, are eaten up with implacable, blood-thirsty rancour against their former lords and owners. The annals of Hayti form quite a cabinet of political and social object-lessons which, in the eyes of British statesmen, should be invaluable in showing the true method of dealing with Ethiopic subjects of the Crown. The Negro race in Hayti, in order to obtain and to guard what it calls its freedom, has outraged every humane instinct and falsified every benevolent hope. The slave-owners there had not been a whit more cruel than slave-owners in the other islands. But, in spite of this, how ferocious, how sanguinary,

how relentless against them has the vengeance
of the Blacks been in their hour of mastery!
A century has passed away since then, and, notwithstanding that, the hatred of Whites still
rankles in their souls, and is cherished and
yielded to as a national creed and guide of
conduct.  Colonial administrators of the mighty
British Empire, the lesson which History has
taught and yet continues to teach you in Hayti
as to the best mode of dealing with your
Ethiopic colonists lies patent, blood-stained and
terrible before you, and should be taken definitively to heart.  But if you are willing that
Civilization and Religion—in short, all the
highest developments of individual and social
life—should at once be swept away by a
desolating vandalism of African birth; if you
do not recoil from the blood-guiltiness that
would stain your consciences through the mas-
sacre of our fellow-countrymen in the West
Indies, on account of their race, complexion and
enlightenment ; finally, if you desire those
modern Hesperides to revert into primeval
jungle, horrent lairs wherein the Blacks, who,
but a short while before, had been ostensibly
civilized, shall be revellers, as high-priests and

devotees, in orgies of devil-worship, cannibalism, and obeah—dare to give the franchise to those West Indian Colonies, and then rue the consequences of your infatuation ! . . .

Alas, if the foregoing summary of the ghastly imaginings of Mr. Froude were true, in what a fool's paradise had the wisest and best amongst us been living, moving, and having our being ! Up to the date of the suggestion by him as above of the alleged facts and possibilities of West Indian life, we had believed (even granting the correctness of his gloomy account of the past and present positions of the two races) that to no well-thinking West Indian White, whose ancestors may have, innocently or culpably, participated in the gains as well as the guilt of slavery, would the remembrance of its palmy days be otherwise than one of regret. We Negroes, on the other hand, after a lapse of time extending over nearly two generations, could be indebted only to precarious tradition or scarcely accessible documents for any knowledge we might chance upon of the sufferings endured in these Islands of the West by those of our race who have gone before us. Death, with undiscriminating hand, had gathered in the human harvest of masters and slaves alike, according to or out of the normal laws of nature ; while Time had been letting down on the stage of our existence drop-scene after drop-scene of years, to the number of something like fifty, which had been curtaining off the tragic incidents of the past from the peaceful activities of the present. Being thus circumstanced, thought we, what rational elements of mutual hatred should *now* continue to exist in the bosoms of the two races ?

With regard to the perpetual reference to Hayti, because of our oneness with its inhabitants in origin and complexion, as a criterion for the exact forecast of our future conduct under given circumstances, this appeared to us, looking at actual facts, perversity gone wild in the manufacture of analogies. The founders of the Black Republic, we had all along understood, were not in any sense whatever equipped, as Mr. Froude assures us they were, when starting on their self-governing career, with the civil and intellectual advantages that had been transplanted from Europe. On the contrary, we had been taught to regard them as most unfortunate in the circumstances under which

they so gloriously conquered their merited freedom. We saw them free, but perfectly illiterate
barbarians, impotent to use the intellectual resources of which their valour had made them
possessors, in the shape of books on the spirit
and technical details of a highly developed
national existence. We had learnt also, until
this new interpreter of history had contradicted
the accepted record, that the continued failure
of Hayti to realize the dreams of Toussaint was
due to the fatal want of confidence subsisting
between the fairer and darker sections of the
inhabitants, which had its sinister and disastrous origin in the action of the Mulattoes in
attempting to secure freedom for themselves,
in conjunction with the Whites, at the sacrifice
of their darker-hued kinsmen. Finally, it had
been explained to us that the remembrance of
this abnormal treason had been underlying and
perniciously influencing the whole course of
Haytian national history. All this established
knowledge we are called upon to throw over-
board, and accept the baseless assertions of
this conjuror-up of inconceivable fables ! He
calls upon us to believe that, in spite of being
free, educated, progressive, and at peace with

all men, we West Indian Blacks, were we ever
to become constitutionally dominant in our
native islands, would emulate in savagery
our Haytian fellow-Blacks who, at the time
of retaliating upon their actual masters, were
tortured slaves, bleeding and rendered desperate
under the oppressors' lash—and all this simply
and merely because of the sameness of our
ancestry and the colour of our skin! One
would have thought that Liberia would have
been a fitter standard of comparison in respect
of a coloured population starting a national life,
really and truly equipped with the requisites
and essentials of civilized existence. But such a
reference would have been fatal to Mr. Froude's
object : the annals of Liberia being a persistent
refutation of the old pro-slavery prophecies
which our author so feelingly rehearses.

Let us revert, however, to Grenada and the
newly-published " Bow of Ulysses," which had
come into my hands in April, 1888.

It seemed to me, on reading that book, and
deducing therefrom the foregoing essential
summary, that a critic would have little more to
do, in order to effectually exorcise this negro-
phobic political hobgoblin, than to appeal to

impartial history, as well as to common sense, in its application to human nature in general, and to the actual facts of West Indian life in particular.

History, as against the hard and fast White-master and Black-slave theory so recklessly invented and confidently built upon by Mr. Froude, would show incontestably—(*a*) that for upwards of two hundred years before the Negro Emancipation, in 1838, there had never existed in one of those then British Colonies, which had been originally discovered and settled for Spain by the great Columbus or by his successors, the *Conquistadores*, any prohibition whatsoever, on the ground of race or colour, against the owning of slaves by any free person possessing the necessary means, and desirous of doing so ; (*b*) that, as a consequence of this non-restriction, and from causes notoriously historical, numbers of blacks, half-breeds, and other non-Europeans, besides such of them as had become possessed of their "property" by inheritance, availed themselves of this virtual license, and in course of time constituted a very considerable proportion of the slave-holding section of those communities; (*c*) that these dusky plantation-owners enjoyed and used in every possible sense the identical rights and privileges which were enjoyed and used by their pure-blooded Caucasian brother-slave-owners. The above statements are attested by written documents, oral tradition, and, better still perhaps, by the living presence in those islands of numerous lineal representatives of those once opulent and flourishing non-European planter-families.

Common sense, here stepping in, must, from the above data, deduce some such conclusions as the following. First that, on the hypothesis that the slaves who were freed in 1838—full fifty years ago—were all on an average fifteen years old, those vengeful ex-slaves of to-day will be all men of sixty-five years of age ; and, allowing for the delay in getting the franchise, somewhat further advanced towards the human life-term of threescore and ten years. Again, in order to organize and carry out any scheme of legislative and social retaliation of the kind set forth in the " Bow of Ulysses," there must be (which unquestionably there is not) a considerable, well-educated, and very influential number surviving of those who had actually been in bondage. Moreover, the vengeance of these people (also assuming the foregoing non-existent condition) would have, in case of opportunity, to wreak itself far more largely and vigorously upon members of their own race than upon Whites, seeing that the increase of the Blacks, as correctly represented in the " Bow of Ulysses," is just as rapid as the diminution of the White population. And therefore, Mr. Froude's " Danger-to-the-Whites " cry in support of his anti-reform manifesto would not appear, after all, to be quite so justifiable as he possibly thinks.

Feeling keenly that something in the shape of the foregoing programme might be successfully worked up for a public defence of the maligned people, I disregarded the bodily and mental obstacles that have beset and clouded my career during the last twelve years, and cheerfully undertook the task, stimulated thereto by what I thought weighty considerations. I saw that no representative of Her Majesty's Ethiopic West Indian subjects cared to come forward to perform this work in the more permanent shape that I felt to be not only desirable but essential for our self-vindication.

I also realized the fact that the " Bow of Ulysses " was not likely to have the same ephemeral existence and effect as the newspaper and other periodical discussions of its contents, which had poured from the press in Great Britain, the United States, and very notably, of course, in all the English Colonies of the Western Hemisphere. In the West Indian papers the best writers of our race had written masterly refutations, but it was clear how difficult the task would be in future to procure and refer to them whenever occasion should require. Such productions, however, fully satisfied those qualified men of our people, because they were legitimately convinced (even as I myself am convinced) that the political destinies of the people of colour could not run one tittle of risk from anything that it pleased Mr. Froude to write or say on the subject. But, meditating further on the question, the reflection forced itself upon me that, beyond the mere political personages in the circle more directly addressed by Mr. Froude's volume, there were individuals whose influence or possible sympathy we could not afford to disregard, or to esteem lightly. So I deemed it right and a patriotic duty to attempt the enterprise myself, in obedience to the above stated motives.

At this point I must pause to express on behalf of the entire coloured population of the West Indies our most heartfelt acknowledgments to Mr. C. Salmon for the luminous and effective vindication of us, in his volume on " West Indian Confederation," against Mr. Froude's libels. The service thus rendered by Mr. Salmon possesses a double significance and value in my estimation. In the first place, as being the work of a European of high position, quite independent of us (who testifies concerning Negroes, not through having gazed at them from balconies, decks of steamers, or the seats of moving carriages, but from actual and long personal intercourse with them, which the internal evidence of his book plainly proves to have been as sympathetic as it was familiar), and, secondly, as the work of an individual entirely outside of our race, it has been gratefully accepted by myself as an incentive to self-help, on the same more formal and permanent lines, in a matter so important to the status which we can justly claim as a progressive, law-abiding, and self-respecting section of Her Majesty's liege subjects.

2

It behoves me now to say a few words respecting this book as a mere literary production.

Alexander Pope, who, next to Shakespeare and perhaps Butler, was the most copious contributor to the current stock of English maxims, says :

> " True ease in writing comes from Art, not Chance,
>     As those move easiest who have learnt to dance."

A whole dozen years of bodily sickness and mental tribulation have not been conducive to that regularity of practice in composition which alone can ensure the "true ease" spoken of by the poet ; and therefore is it that my style leaves so much to be desired, and exhibits, perhaps, still more to be pardoned.  Happily, a quarrel such as ours with the author of " The English in the West Indies " cannot be finally or even approximately settled on the score of superior literary competency, whether of aggressor or defender.  I feel free to ignore whatever verdict might be grounded on a consideration so purely artificial.  There ought to be enough, if not in these pages, at any rate in whatever else I have heretofore published, that should prove me not so hopelessly stupid and wanting in

self-respect, as would be implied by my under-
taking a contest in artistic phrase-weaving with
one who, even among the foremost of his
literary countrymen, is confessedly a master in
that craft.  The judges to whom I do submit
our case are those Englishmen and others
whose conscience blends with their judgment,
and who determine such questions as this on
their essential rightness which has claim to the
first and decisive consideration.  For much that
is irregular in the arrangement and sequence of
the subject-matter, some blame fairly attaches to
our assailant.  The erratic manner in which he
launches his injurious statements against the
hapless Blacks, even in the course of passages
which no more led up to them than to any
other section of mankind, is a very notable
feature of his anti-Negro production.  As he
frequently repeats, very often with cynical
aggravations, his charges and sinister prophecies against the sable objects of his aversion,
I could see no other course open to me than to
take him up on the points whereto I demurred,
exactly how, when, and where I found them.

My purpose could not be attained up without
direct mention of, or reference to, certain public

employés in the Colonies whose official conduct
has often been the subject of criticism in the
public press of the West Indies.   Though fully
aware that such criticism has on many occasions
been much more severe than my own strictures,
yet, it being possible that some special responsibility may attach to what I here reproduce in a
more permanent shape, I most cheerfully accept,
in the interests of public justice, any consequence
which may result.

A remark or two concerning the publication
of this rejoinder.   It has been hinted to me that
the issue of it has been too long delayed to
secure for it any attention in England, owing
to the fact that the West Indies are but little
known, and of less interest, to the generality of
English readers.   Whilst admitting, as in duty
bound, the possible correctness of this forecast, and regretting the oft-recurring hindrances
which occasioned such frequent and, sometimes, long suspension of my labour ; and
noting, too, the additional delay caused through
my unacquaintance with English publishing
usages, I must, notwithstanding, plead guilty
to a lurking hope that some small fraction
of Mr. Froude's readers will yet be found,

whose interest in the West Indies will be
temporarily revived on behalf of this essay,
owing to its direct bearing on Mr. Froude and
his statements relative to these Islands, con
tained in his recent book of travels in them.
This I am led to hope will be more particularly
the case when it is borne in mind that the
rejoinder has been attempted by a member of
that very same race which he has, with such
eloquent recklessness of all moral considerations,
held up to public contempt and disfavour. In
short, I can scarcely permit myself to believe it
possible that concern regarding a popular author,
on his being questioned by an adverse critic
of however restricted powers, can be so utterly
dead within a twelvemonth as to be incapable
of rekindling. Mr. Froude's " Oceana," which
had been published long before its author
voyaged to the West Indies, in order to treat
the Queen's subjects there in the same more
than questionable fashion as that in which he
had treated those of the Southern Hemisphere,
had what was in the main a formal rejoinder
to its misrepresentations published only three
months ago in this city. I venture to believe
that no serious work in defence of an impor-

tant cause or community can lose much, if anything, of its intrinsic value through some delay in its issue ; especially when written in the vindication of Truth, whose eternal principles are beyond and above the influence of time and its changes.

At any rate, this attempt to answer some of Mr. Froude's main allegations against the people of the West Indies cannot fail to be of grave importance and lively interest to the inhabitants of those Colonies. In this opinion I am happy in being able to record the full concurrence of a numerous and influential body of my fellow-West Indians, men of various races, but united in detestation of falsehood and injustice.

J. J. T.

LONDON, *June*, 1889.

# Contents.

## BOOK I.

BOOK I.

# INTRODUCTION.

———◆———

LIKE the ancient hero, one of whose warlike equipments furnishes the complementary title of his book, the author of " The English in the West Indies ; or, The Bow of Ulysses," sallied forth from his home to study, if not cities, at least men (especially *black* men), and their manners in the British Antilles.

James Anthony Froude is, beyond any doubt whatever, a very considerable figure in modern English literature. It has, however, for some time ceased to be a question whether his acceptability, to the extent which it reaches, has not been due rather to the verbal attractiveness than to the intrinsic value and trustworthiness of his opinions and teachings. In fact, so far as a judgment can be formed from examined specimens of his writings, it appears that our

author is the bond-slave of his own phrases.
To secure an artistic perfection of style, he dis-
regards all obstacles, not only those presented
by the requirements of verity, but such as
spring from any other kind of consideration
whatsoever. The doubt may safely be entertained whether, among modern British men
of letters, there be one of equal capability who,
in the interest of the happiness of his sentences,
so cynically sacrifices what is due not only to
himself as a public instructor, but also to that
public whom he professes to instruct. Yet, as
the too evident plaything of an over-permeable
moral constitution, he might set up some plea in
explanation of his ethical vagaries. He might
urge, for instance, that the high culture of which
his books are all so redolent has utterly failed
to imbue him with the *nil admirari* sentiment,
which Horace commends as the sole specific
for making men happy and keeping them so.
For, as a matter of fact, and with special
reference to the work we have undertaken to
discuss, Mr. Froude, though cynical in his
general utterances regarding Negroes—of the
male sex, be it noted—is, in the main, all extravagance and self-abandonment whenever he

brings an object of his arbitrary likes or dislikes under discussion. At such times he is no observer, much less worshipper, of proportion in his delineations. Thorough-paced, scarcely controllable, his enthusiasm for or against admits no degree in its expression, save and except the superlative. Hence Mr. Froude's statement of facts or description of phenomena, whenever his feelings are enlisted either way, must be taken with the proverbial "grain of salt" by all when enjoying the luxury of perusing his books. So complete is his self-identification with the sect or individual for the time being engrossing his sympathy, that even their personal antipathies are made his own; and the hostile language, often exaggerated and unjust, in which those antipathies find vent, secures in his more chastened mode of utterance an exact reproduction none the less injurious because divested of grossness.

Of this special phase of self-manifestation a typical instance is afforded at page 164, under the heading of "Dominica," in a passage which at once embraces and accentuates the whole spirit and method of the work. To a eulogium of the professional skill and suc-

cessful agricultural enterprise of Dr. Nichol,
a medical officer of that Colony, with whom he
became acquainted for the first time during his
short stay there, our author travels out of his
way to tack on a gratuitous and pointless sneer
at the educational competency of all the elected
members of the island legislature, among whom,
he tells us, the worthy doctor had often tried
in vain to obtain a place. His want of
success, our author informs his readers, was
brought about through Dr. Nichol " being the
*only* man in the Colony of superior attainments."
Persons acquainted with the stormy politics of
that lovely little island do not require to be
informed that the bitterest animosity had for
years been raging between Dr. Nichol and
some of the elected members—a fact which
our author chose characteristically to regard as
justifying an onslaught by himself on the whole
of that section of which the foes of his new
friend formed a prominent part.

Swayed by the above specified motives, our
author also manages to see much that is, and
always has been, invisible to mortal eye, and
to fail to hear what is audible to and remarked
upon by every other observer.

Thus we find him (p. 56) describing the Grenada Carenage as being surrounded by forest trees, causing its waters to present a violet tint ; whilst every one familiar with that locality knows that there are no forest trees within two miles of the object which they are so ingeniously made to colour. Again, and aptly illustrating the influence of his prejudices on his sense of hearing, we will notice somewhat more in detail the following assertion respecting the speech of the gentry of Barbados :—

"The language of the Anglo-Barbadians was pure English, the voices without the smallest transatlantic intonation."

Now it so happens that no Barbadian born and bred, be he gentle or simple, can, on opening his lips, avoid the fate of Peter of Galilee when skulking from the peril of a detected nationality : "Thy speech bewrayeth thee !" It would, however, be prudent on this point to take the evidence of other Englishmen, whose testimony is above suspicion, seeing that they were free from the moral disturbance that affected Mr. Froude's auditory powers. G. J. Chester, in his "Transatlantic Sketches" (page 95), deposes as follows :—

"But worse, far worse than the colour, both of men and women, is their *voice and accent.* Well may Coleridge enumerate among the pains of the West Indies, 'the *yawny-drawny* way in which men converse.' The soft, whining drawl is simply intolerable. Resemble the worst Northern States woman's accent it may in some degree, but it has not a grain of its vigour. A man tells you, 'if you can *speer* it, to send a *beerer* with a bottle of *bare,*' and the clergyman excruciates you by praying in church, '*Speer* us, good Lord.' The English pronunciation of A and E is in most words transposed. Barbados has a considerable number of provincialisms of dialect. Some of these, as the constant use of "Mistress" for 'Mrs.,' are interesting as archaisms, or words in use in the early days of the Colony, and which have never died out of use. Others are Yankeeisms or vulgarisms ; others, again, such as the expression 'turning cuffums,' *i.e.* summersets, from cuffums, a species of fish, seem to be of local origin."

In a note hereto appended, the author gives a list of English words of peculiar use and acceptation in Barbados.

To the same effect writes Anthony Trollope:
" But if the black people differ from their
brethren of the other islands, so certainly do
the white people. One soon learns to know—
a Bim. That is the name in which they themselves delight, and therefore, though there is
a sound of slang about it, I give it here. One
certainly soon learns to know a Bim. The
most peculiar distinction *is in his voice.* There
is *always a nasal twang about it,* but quite
distinct from the nasality of a Yankee. The
Yankee's word rings sharp through his nose ;
not so that of the first-class Bim. There is
a soft drawl about it, and the sound is seldom
completely formed. The effect on the ear is
the same as that on the hand when a man gives
you his to shake, and instead of shaking yours,
holds his own still, &c., &c." (" The West
Indies," p. 207).

From the above and scores of other authori-
tative testimonies which might have been cited
to the direct contrary of our traveller's tale
under this head, we can plainly perceive
that Mr. Froude's love is not only blind, but
adder-deaf as well. We shall now contemplate
him under circumstances where his feelings are
quite other than those of a partisan.

VOYAGE OUT.

That Mr. Froude, despite his professions to the contrary, did not go out on his explorations unhampered by prejudices, seems clear enough from the following quotation :—

"There was a small black boy among us, evidently of pure blood, for his hair was wool and his colour black as ink. His parents must have been well-to-do, for the boy had been to Europe to be educated. The officers on board and some of the ladies played with him as they would play with a monkey. He had little more sense than a monkey, perhaps less, and the gestures of him grinning behind gratings and perching out his long thin arms between the bars were curiously suggestive of the original from whom we are told now that all of us came. The worst of it was that, being lifted above his own people, he had been taught to despise them. He was spoilt as a black and could not be made into a white, and this I found afterwards was the invariable and dangerous consequence whenever a superior negro contrived to raise himself. He might do well enough himself, but his family feel their blood as degradation. His

children will not marry among their own people,
and not only will no white girl marry a negro,
but hardly any dowry can be large enough to
tempt a West Indian white to make a wife of
a black lady. This is one of the most sinister
features in the present state of social life there."

We may safely assume that the playing of
" the officers on board and some of the ladies "
with the boy, "as they would play with a
monkey," is evidently a suggestion of Mr.
Froude's own soul, as well as the resemblance
to the simian tribe which he makes out from
the frolics of the lad. Verily, it requires an
eye rendered more than microscopic by prejudice to discern the difference between the gam-
bols of juveniles of any colour under similar
conditions. It is true that it might just be
the difference between the friskings of white
lambs and the friskings of lambs that are not
white. That any black pupil should be *taught*
to despise his own people through being lifted
above them by education, seems a reckless
statement, and far from patriotic withal ; inasmuch as the education referred to here was
European, and the place from which it was
obtained presumably England. At all events,

the difference among educated black men in deportment towards their unenlightened fellow-blacks, can be proved to have nothing of that cynicism which often marks the bearing of Englishmen in an analogous case with regard to their less favoured countrymen. The statement that a black person can be " spoilt " for such by education, whilst he cannot be made white, is one of the silly conceits which the worship of the skin engenders in ill-conditioned minds. No sympathy should be wasted on the negro sufferer from mortification at not being able to " change his skin." The Ethiopian of whatever shade of colour who is not satisfied with being such was never intended to be more than a mere living figure. Mr. Froude further confidently states that whilst a superior Negro " might do well himself," yet " his family feel their blood as a degradation." If there be some who so feel, they are indeed very much to be pitied ; but their sentiments are not entitled to the serious importance with which our critic has invested them. But is it at all conceivable that a people whose sanity has never in any way been questioned would strain every nerve to secure for their offspring a distinction the consequence of which to themselves would be a feeling of their own abasement? The poor Irish peasant who toils and starves to secure for his eldest son admission into the Catholic priesthood, has a far other feeling than one of humiliation when contemplating that son eventually as the spiritual director of a congregation and parish. Similarly, the laudable ambition which, in the case of a humble Scotch matron, is expressed in the wish and exertion to see her Jamie or Geordie "wag his pow in the pou'pit," produces, when realized, salutary effects in the whole family connection. These effects, which Mr. Froude would doubtless allow and commend in their case, he finds it creditable to ignore the very possibility of in the experience of people whose cuticle is not white. It is, however, but bare justice to say that, as Negroes are by no means deficient in self-love and the tenderness of natural affection, such gratifying fulfilment of a family's hopes exerts an elevating and, in many cases, an ennobling influence on every one connected with the fortunate household. Nor, from the eminently sympathetic nature of the African race, are the near friends of a family

unbenefited in a similar way.   This is true, and
distinctively human ; but, naturally, no apolo-
gist of Negro depreciation would admit the
reasonableness of applying to the affairs of
Negroes the principles of common equity, or
even of common sense.   To sum up practically
our argument on this head, we shall suppose
West Indians to be called upon to imagine that
the less distinguished relations respectively of,
say, the late Solicitor-General of Trinidad and
the present Chief Justice of Barbados could
be otherwise than legitimately elated at the
conspicuous position won by a member of their
own household.

Mr. Froude further ventures to declare, in this
connection, that the children of educated coloured
folk " will not marry among their own people."
Will he tell us, then, whom the daughters
marry, or if they ever do marry at all, since he
asserts, with regard to West Indian Whites, that
"hardly any dowry can be large enough to
tempt them to make a wife of a black lady " ?
Our author evidently does not feel or care that
the suggestion he here induces is a hideous
slander against a large body of respectable people
of whose affairs he is absolutely ignorant.   Full

of the "go" imparted to his talk by a consciousness of absolute license with regard to Negroes,
our dignified narrator makes the parenthetical
assertion that no white girl (in the West
Indies) will "marry a Negro." But has he
been informed that cases upon cases have
occurred in those Colonies, and in very high
"Anglo-West Indian" families too, where the
social degradation of being *married* to Negroes
has been avoided by the alternative of forming
base private connections even with menials of
that race ?

The marrying of a black wife, on the other
hand, by a West Indian White was an event of
frequent occurrence at a period in regard to
which our historian seems to be culpably un-
informed. In slavery days, when all planters,
black and white alike, were fused in a common
solidarity of interests, the skin-distinction
which Mr. Froude so strenuously advocates,
and would fain risk so much to promote, did
not, so far as matrimony was concerned, exist
in the degree that it now does. Self-interest
often dictated such unions, especially on the
part of in-coming Whites desiring to strengthen
their position and to increase their influence in

the land of their adoption by means of advan-
tageous Creole marriages.　Love, too, sheer
uncalculating love, impelled not a few Whites to
enter the hymeneal state with the dusky cap-
tivators of their affections.　When rich, the
white planter not seldom paid for such gratification of his laudable impulse by accepting
exclusion from " Society "—and when poor, he
incurred almost invariably his dismissal from
employment.　Of course, in all cases of the
sort the dispensers of such penalties were
actuated by high motives which, nevertheless,
did not stand in the way of their meeting, in
the households of the persons thus obnoxious
to punishment, the same or even a lower
class of Ethiopic damsels, under the title of
"housekeeper," on whom they lavished a
very plethora of caresses.　Perhaps it may be
wrong so to hint it, but, judging from indications in his own book, our author himself would
have been liable in those days to enthralment
by the piquant charms that proved irresistible
to so many of his brother-Europeans.　It is
almost superfluous to repeat that the skin-
discriminating policy induced as regards the
coloured subjects of the Queen since the

abolition of slavery did not, and could not, operate when coloured and white stood on the same high level as slave-owners and ruling potentates in the Colonies. Of course, when the administrative power passed entirely into the hands of British officials, their colonial compatriots coalesced with them, and found no loss in being in the good books of the dominant personages.

In conclusion of our remarks upon the above extracts, it may be stated that the blending of the races is not a burning question. " It can keep," as Mr. Bright wittily said with regard to a subject of similar urgency. Time and Nature might safely be left uninterfered with to work out whatever social development of this kind is in store for the world and its inhabitants.

### BARBADOS.

Our distinguished voyager visited many of the British West Indies, landing first at Barbados, his social experience whereof is set forth in a very agreeable account. Our immediate business, however, is not with what West Indian hospitality, especially among the well-to-do classes, can and does accomplish for

the entertainment of visitors, and particularly
visitors so eminent as Mr. Froude. We are
concerned with what Mr. Froude has to say
concerning our dusky brethren and sisters in
those Colonies. We have, thus, much pleasure
in being able at the outset to extract the
following favourable verdict of his respecting
them—premising, at the same time, that the
balcony from which Mr. Froude surveyed the
teeming multitude in Bridgetown was that of
a grand hotel at which he had, on invitation,
partaken of the refreshing beverage mentioned
in the citation :—

"Cocktail over, and walking in the heat of the
sun being a thing not to be thought of, I sat for
two hours in the balcony, watching the people,
who were as thick as bees in swarming time.
Nine-tenths of them were pure black. You
rarely saw a white face, but still less would you
see a discontented one, imperturbable good
humour and self-satisfaction being written on
the features of every one. The women struck
me especially. They were smartly dressed in
white calico, scrupulously clean, and tricked out
with ribands and feathers ; but their figures
were so good, and they carried themselves so

well and gracefully, that although they might make themselves absurd, they could not look vulgar. Like the Greek and Etruscan women, they are trained from childhood to carry weights on their heads. They are thus perfectly upright, and plant their feet firmly and naturally on the ground. They might serve for sculptors' models, and are well aware of it."

Regarding the other sex, Mr. Froude says:—

"The men were active enough, driving carts, wheeling barrows, and selling flying-fish," &c.

He also speaks with candour of the entire absence of drunkenness and quarrelling, and the agreeable prevalence of good humour and light-heartedness among them. Some critic might, on reading the above extract from our author's account of the men, be tempted to ask—"But what is the meaning of that little word 'enough' occurring therein?" We should be disposed to hazard a suggestion that Mr. Froude, being fair-minded and loyal to truth, as far as is compatible with his sympathy for his hapless "Anglo-West Indians," could not give an entirely ungrudging testimony in favour of the possible, nay probable, voters by whose suffrages the supremacy of the Dark

Parliament will be ensured, and the relapse into obeahism, devil-worship, and children-eating be inaugurated. Nevertheless, *Si sic omnia dixisset*—if he had said all things thus! Yes, if Mr. Froude had, throughout his volume, spoken in this strain, his occasional want of patience and fairness with regard to our male kindred might have found condonation in his even more than chivalrous appreciation of our womankind. But it has been otherwise. So we are forced to try conclusions with him in the arena of his own selection—unreflecting spokesman that he is of British colonialism, which, we grieve to learn through Mr. Froude's pages, has, like the Bourbon family, not only forgotten nothing, but, unfortunately for its own peace, learnt nothing also.

ST. VINCENT.

The following are the words in which our traveller embodies the main motive and purpose of his voyage :—

" My own chief desire was to see the human inhabitants, to learn what they were doing, how they were living, and what they were thinking about. . . ."

But, alas, with the mercurialism of temperament in which he has thought proper to
indulge when only Negroes and Europeans
not of "Anglo-West Indian" tendencies were
concerned, he jauntily threw to the winds all
the scruples and cautious minuteness which were
essential to the proper execution of his project.
At Barbados, as we have seen, he satisfies
himself with sitting aloft, at a balcony-window,
to contemplate the movements of the sable
throng below, of whose character, moral and
political, he nevertheless professes to have
become a trustworthy delineator. From the
above-quoted account of his impressions of the
external traits and deportment of the Ethiopic
folk thus superficially gazed at, our author
passes on to an analysis of their mental
and moral idiosyncrasies, and other intimate
matters, which the very silence of the book
as to his method of ascertaining them is a
sufficent proof that his knowledge in their
regard has not been acquired directly and at
first hand. Nor need we say that the generally adverse cast of his verdicts on what he had
been at no pains to study for himself points
to the "hostileness" of the witnesses whose

testimony alone has formed the basis of his conclusions. Throughout Mr. Froude's tour in the British Colonies his intercourse was exclusively with " Anglo-West Indians," whose aversion to the Blacks he has himself, perhaps they would think indiscreetly, placed on record. In no instance do we find that he condescended to visit the abode of any Negro, whether it was the mansion of a gentleman or the hut of a peasant of that race. The whole tenor of the book indicates his rigid adherence to this onesided course, and suggests also that, as a traveller, Mr. Froude considers maligning on hearsay to be just as convenient as reporting facts elicited by personal investigation. Proceed we, however, to strengthen our statement regarding his definitive abandonment, and that without any apparent reason, of the plan he had professedly laid down for himself at starting, and failing which no trustworthy data could have been obtained concerning the character and disposition of the people about whom he undertakes to thoroughly enlighten his readers. Speaking of St. Vincent, where he arrived immediately after leaving Barbados, our author says :—

"I did not land,.for the time was short, and as a beautiful picture the island was best seen from the deck. The characteristics of the people are the same in all the Antilles, and could be studied elsewhere."

Now, it is a fact, patent and notorious, that "the characteristics of the people are" *not* "the same in all the Antilles." A man of Mr. Froude's attainments, whose studies have made him familiar with ethnological facts, must be aware that difference of local surroundings and influences does, in the course of time, inevitably create difference of characteristic and deportment. Hence there is in nearly every Colony a marked dissimilarity of native qualities amongst the Negro inhabitants, arising not only from the causes above indicated, but largely also from the great diversity of their African ancestry. We might as well be told that because the nations of Europe are generally white and descended from Japhet, they could be studied one by the light derived from acquaintance with another. We venture to declare that, unless a common education from youth has been shared by them, the Hamitic inhabitants of one island have very little in common with those of another, beyond the dusky skin and woolly hair. In speech, character, and deportment, a coloured native of Trinidad differs as much from one of Barbados as a North American black does from either, in all the above respects.

In Grenada, the next island he arrived at, our traveller's procedure with regard to the inhabitants was very similar. There he landed in the afternoon, drove three or four miles inland to dine at the house of a "gentleman who was a passing resident," returned in the dark to his ship, and started for Trinidad. In the course of this journey back, however, as he sped along in the carriage, Mr. Froude found opportunity to look into the people's houses along the way, where, he tells us, he "could see and was astonished to observe signs of comfort, and even signs of taste—armchairs, sofas, side-boards with cut-glass upon them, engravings and coloured prints upon the walls." As a result of this nocturnal examination, *à vol d'oiseau*, he has written paragraph upon paragraph about the people's character

and prospects in the island of Grenada. To
read the patronizing terms in which our
historian-traveller has seen fit to comment on
Grenada and its people, one would believe
that his account is of some half-civilized, out-
of-the-way region under British sway, and
inhabited chiefly by a horde of semi-barbarian
ignoramuses of African descent. If the world
had not by this time thoroughly assessed the
intrinsic value of Mr. Froude's utterances, one
who knows Grenada might have felt inclined
to resent his causeless depreciation of the
intellectual capacity of its inhabitants ; but considering the estimate which has been pretty
generally formed of his historical judgment,
Mr. Froude may be dismissed, as regards
Grenada and its people, with a certain degree
of scepticism. Such scepticism, though lost
upon himself, is unquestionably needful to protect his readers from the hallucination which
the author's singular contempt for accuracy is
but too liable to induce.

Those who know Grenada and its affairs
are perfectly familiar with the fact that all of
its chief intellectual business, whether official
(even in the highest degree, such as temporary

administration of the government), legal, commercial, municipal, educational, or journalistic,
has been for years upon years carried on by
men of colour.  And what, as a consequence
of this fact, has the world ever heard in dis-
paragement of Grenada throughout this long
series of years ?  Assuredly not a syllable.  On
the contrary, she has been the theme of praise,
not only for the admirable foresight with which
she avoided the sugar crisis, so disastrous to
her sister islands, but also for the pluck and
persistence shown in sustaining herself through
an agricultural emergency brought about by
commercial reverses, whereby the steady march
of her sons in self-advancement was only
checked for a time, but never definitively
arrested.  In fine, as regards every branch of
civilized employment pursued there, the good
people of Grenada hold their own so well and
worthily that any show of patronage, even from
a source more entitled to confidence, would
simply be a piece of obtrusive kindness, not
acceptable to any, seeing that it is required by
none.

BOOK II.

# TRINIDAD.

———•◦•———

MR. FROUDE, crossing the ninety miles of the Caribbean Sea lying between Grenada and Trinidad, lands next morning in Port of Spain, the chief city of that "splendid colony," as Governor Irving, its worst ruler, truly calls it in his farewell message to the Legislature. Regarding Port of Spain in particular, Mr. Froude is positively exuberant in the display of the peculiar qualities that distinguish him, and which we have already admitted. Ecstatic praise and groundless detraction go hand in hand, bewildering to any one not possessed of the key to the mystery of the art of blow-ing hot and cold, which Mr. Froude so start-lingly exemplifies. As it is our purpose to make what he says concerning this Colony the crucial test of his veracity as a writer of travels, and also of the value of his judgments respecting men and things, we shall first invite the reader's attention to the following extracts, with our discussion thereof :—

" On landing we found ourselves in a large foreign-looking town, Port of Spain having been built by French and Spaniards according to their national tendencies, and especially with a view to the temperature, which is that of a forcing house, and rarely falls below 80°. The streets are broad, and are planted with trees for shade, each house where room permits having a garden of its own, with palms and mangoes and coffee-plants and creepers. *Of sanitary arrangements there seemed to be none.* There is abundance of rain, and the gutters which run down by the footway are flushed almost every day. But they are all open. Dirt of every kind lies about freely, to be washed into them *or left to putrify as fate shall direct* " (p. 64).

Lower down, on the same page, our author, luxuriating in his contempt for exactitude when the character of other folk only is at stake, continues :—" The town has between thirty and forty thousand people living in it, *and the*

*rain and Johnny crows between them keep off
pestilence.*" On page 65 we have the following
astounding statement with respect to one of the
trees in the garden in front of the house in
which Mr. Froude was sojourning :—" At the
gate stood as sentinel a cabbage palm *a
hundred feet high.*"

The above quotations, in which we have
elected to be content with indicating by typo-
graphical differences the points on which attention should be mostly directed, will suffice, with
any one knowing Trinidad, as examples of Mr.
Froude's trustworthiness. But as these are
only on matters of mere detail, involving no
question of principle, they are dismissed without any further comment. It must not be so,
however, with the following remarkable de-
liverances which occur on page 67 of his too
picturesque work :—" The commonplace in-
trudes upon the imaginative. At moments one
can fancy that the world is an enchanted place
after all, but then comes generally an absurd
awakening. On the first night of my arrival,
before we went to bed, there came an invitation
to me to attend a political meeting which was
to be held in a few days on the Savannah.

Trinidad is *a purely Crown colony*, and has
escaped hitherto the introduction of *the election
virus.* The newspapers *and certain busy
gentlemen* in Port of Spain had discovered
that they were living under a 'degrading
tyranny,' and they demanded a constitution.
*They did not complain that their affairs had
been ill-managed.* On the contrary, they insisted that they were the most prosperous of
the West Indian colonies, and alone had a
surplus in their treasury. If this was so, it
seemed to me that they had better let well
alone. The population, all told, *was but*
170,000, *less by thirty thousand than that of
Barbados.* They were a mixed and motley
assemblage of all races and colours, busy each
with their own affairs, *and never hitherto
troubling themselves about politics.* But it
had pleased the Home Government to set
up the beginning of a constitution again in
Jamaica ; *no one knew why,* but so it was ; and
Trinidad did not choose to be behindhand.
The official appointments were valuable, and
had been hitherto given away by the Crown.
The local popularities *very naturally* wished
to have them for themselves. This was the

reality in the thing, so far as there was a
reality. It was dressed up in the phrases
borrowed from the great English masters of
the art, about privileges of manhood, moral
dignity, the elevating influence of the suffrage,
&c., intended for home consumption among the
believers in the orthodox radical faith."

The passages which we have signalized in
the above quotation, and which occur with more
elaboration and heedless assurance on a later
page, will produce a feeling of wonder at the
hardihood of him who not only conceived, but
penned and dared to publish them as well,
against the gentlemen whom we all know to be
be foremost in the political agitation at which
Mr. Froude so flippantly sneers. An emphatic
denial may be opposed to his pretence that
"they did not complain that their affairs had
been ill-managed." Why, the very gist and
kernel of the whole agitation, set forth in print
through long years of iteration, has been the
scandalous mismanagement of the affairs of the
Colony—especially under the baleful administration of Governor Irving. The Augëan
Stable, miscalled by him "The Public Works
Department," and whose officials he coolly

fastened upon the financial vitals of that long-suffering Colony, baffled even the resolute will of a Des Vœux to cleanse it. Poor Sir Sanford Freeling attempted the cleansing, but foundered ignominiously almost as soon as he embarked on that Herculean enterprise. Sir A. E. Havelock, who came after, must be mentioned by the historian of Trinidad merely as an incarnate accident in the succession of Governors to whom the destinies of that maltreated Colony have been successively intrusted since the departure of Sir Arthur Hamilton Gordon. The present Governor of Trinidad, Sir William Robinson, is a man of spirit and intelligence, keenly alive to the grave responsibilities resting on him as a ruler of men and moulder of men's destinies. Has he, with all his energy, his public spirit and indisputable devotion to the furtherance of the Colony's interests, been able to grapple successfully with the giant evil ? Has he effectually gained the ear of our masters in Downing Street regarding the inefficiency and wastefulness of Governor Irving's pet department ? We presume that his success has been but very partial, for otherwise it is difficult to conceive the motive for

retaining the army of officials radiating from
that office, with the chief under whose super-
vision so many architectural and other scandals
have for so long been the order of the day.
The Public Works Department is costly enough
to have been a warning to the whole of the
West Indies. It is true that the lavish squandering of the people's money by that department has been appreciably checked since the
advent of the present head of the Government.
The papers no longer team with accounts, nor is
even the humblest æsthetic sense offended now,
as formerly, with views of unsightly, useless and
flimsy erections, the cost of which, on an average, was five times more than that of good
and reputable structures.

This, however, has been entirely due to
the personal influence of the Governor. Sir
William Robinson, not being the tool, as Sir
Henry Irving owned that he was, of the
Director of Public Works, could not be expected to be his accomplice or screener in the
cynical waste of the public funds. Here, then,
is the personal rectitude of a ruler operating
as a safeguard to the people's interests; and
we gladly confess our entire agreement with

Mr. Froude on the subject of the essential qualifications of a Crown Governor.  Mr. Froude
contends, and we heartily coincide with  him,
that a ruler of high training and noble purposes
would, as the embodiment of the administrative
authority, be  the  very  best  provision  for  the
government of Colonies constituted as ours are.
But  he  has  also  pointed  out,  and  that  in  no
equivocal terms, that the  above  are  far  from
having been indispensable qualifications for  the
patronage of Downing Street.   He has shown
that the  Colonial Office is,  more  often  than
otherwise,  swayed  in  the  appointment  of
Colonial Governors  by  considerations among
which the special fitness of the man appointed
holds but a secondary place.   On this point we
have much gratification in giving Mr. Froude's
own words (p. 91) :—" Among the public servants of Great Britain there are persons always
to be found fit and willing for posts of honour
and difficulty if a sincere effort be made to find
them.  Alas! in  times  past  we  have  sent
persons  to  rule  our  Baratarias  to  whom
Sancho  Panza  was  a  sage — troublesome
members  of  Parliament,  younger  brothers  of
powerful  families,  impecunious  peers ;  favour-

ites, with backstairs influence, for whom a
provision was to be found ; colonial clerks
bred in the office who had been obsequious
and useful !" Now then, applying these facts
to the political history of Trinidad, with which
we are more particularly concerned at present,
what do we find ? We find that in the person
of Sir A. H. Gordon (1867-1870) that Colony at
length chanced upon a ruler both competent
and eager to advance her interests, not only
materially, but in the nobler respects that give
dignity to the existence of a community. Of
course, he was opposed—ably, strenuously, violently, virulently—but the metal of which the
man was composed was only fused into greater
firmness by being subjected to such fiery
tests. On leaving Trinidad, this eminent ruler
left as legacies to the Colony he had loved
and worked for so heartily, laws that placed
the persons and belongings of the inhabitants
beyond the reach of wanton aggression ; the
means by which honest and laborious industry
could, through agriculture, benefit both itself
and the general revenue. He also left an
educational system that opened (to even the
humblest) a free pathway to knowledge, to

distinction, and, if the objects of its beneficence were worthy of the boon, to serviceableness to their native country. Above all, he left peace among the jarring interests which, under the badge of Englishman and of Creole, under the badge of Catholic and under the badge of Protestant, and so many other forms of sectional divergence, had too long distracted Trinidad. This he had effected, not by constituting himself a partisan of either section, but by inquiring with statesmanlike appreciation, and allowing the legitimate claims of each to a certain scope of influence in the furtherance of the Colony's welfare. Hence the bitter rivalry of jarring interests was transformed into harmonious co-operation on all sides, in advancing the common good of the common country.

The Colonial Office, knowing little and caring less about that noble jewel in the British Crown, sent out as successor to so brilliant and successful an administrator—whom ? One Sir James Robert Longden, a gentleman without initiative, without courage, and, above all, with a slavish adherence to red-tape and a clerk-like dread of compromising his berth. Having served for a long series of years in subordinate posts in

minor dependencies, the habit of being impressed and influenced by colonial magnates
grew and gathered strength within him. Such
a ruler, of course, the serpents that had only
been "scotched, but not killed," by the stern pro-
cedures of Governor Gordon, could wind round,
beguile, and finally cause to fall. Measure
after measure of his predecessor which he could
in any way neutralize in the interests of the
colonial clique, was rendered of none effect. In
fact, he was subservient to the wishes of those
who had all long objected to those measures,
but had not dared even to hint their objections
to the beneficent autocrat who had willed and
given them effect for the general welfare.
After Governor Longden came Sir Henry
Turner Irving, a personage who brought to
Trinidad a reputation for all the vulgar colonial
prejudices which, discreditable enough in ordinary folk, are, in the Governor of a mixed
community, nothing less than calamitous.
More than amply did he justify the evil reports
with which rumour had heralded his coming.
Abler, more astute, more daring than Sir James
Longden, who was, on the whole, only a constitutionally timid man, Governor Irving threw

himself heart and soul into the arms of the
Sugar Interest, by whom he had been helped
into his high office, and whose belief he evidently shared, that sugar-growers alone should
be possessors of the lands of the West Indies.
It would be wearisome to detail the methods
by which every act of Sir Arthur Gordon's to
benefit the whole population was cynically and
systematically undone by this his native-hating
successor.  In short, the policy of reaction which
Sir James Longden began, found in Governor
Irving not only a consistent promoter, but, as it
were, a sinister incarnation.  It is true that he
could not, at the bidding and on the advice of
his planter-friends, shut up the Crown Lands
of the Colony against purchasers of limited
means, because they happened to be mostly
natives of colour, but he could annul the provision by which every Warden in the rural
districts, on the receipt of the statutory fees,
had to supply a Government title on the spot to
every one who purchased any acreage of Crown
Lands.  Every intending purchaser, therefore,
whether living at Toco, Guayaguayare, Monos,
or Icacos, the four extreme points of the Island
of Trinidad, was compelled to go to Port of

Spain, forty or fifty miles distant, through an almost roadless country, to compete at the Sub-Intendant's auction sales, with every probability of being outbid in the end, and having his long-deposited money returned to him after all his pains. Lieutenant-Governor Des Vœux told the Legislature of Trinidad that the monstrous Excise imposts of the Colony were an incentive to smuggling, and he thought that the duties, licenses, &c., should be lowered in the interest of good and equitable government. Sir Henry Turner Irving, however, besides raising the duties on spirituous liquors, also enacted that every distillery, however small, must pay a salary to a Government official stationed within it to supervise the manufacture of the spirits. This, of course, was the death-blow to all the minor competition which had so long been disturbing the peace of mind of the mighty possessors of the great distilleries. Ahab was thus made glad with the vineyard of Naboth.

In the matter of official appointments, too, Governor Irving was consistent in his ostentatious hostility to Creoles in general, and to coloured Creoles in particular. Of the fifty-six appointments which that model Go-

5

vernor made in 1876, only seven happened to
be natives and coloured, out of a population in
which the latter element is so preponderant as
to excite the fears of Mr. Froude. In educational
matters, though he could not with any show of
sense or decency re-enact the rule which ex-
cluded students of illegitimate birth from the
advantages of the Royal College, he could,
nevertheless, pander to the prejudices of himself and his friends by raising the standard of
proficiency while reducing the limit of the age
for free admission to that institution—boys of
African descent having shown an irrepressible
persistency in carrying off prizes.

Every one acquainted with Trinidad politics
knows very well the ineffably low dodges
and subterfuges under which the Arima
Railway was prevented from having its terminus in the centre of that town. The public
was promised a saving of Eight Thousand
Pounds by their high-minded Governor for a
diversion of the line "by only a *few yards*" from
the originally projected terminus. In the end
it was found out not only that the terminus of
the railway was nearly a whole mile outside
of the town of Arima, but also that Twenty

Thousand Pounds " Miscellaneous " had to be paid up by the good folk of Trinidad, in addition to gulping down their disappointment at saving no Eight Thousand Pounds, and having to find by bitter experience, especially in rainy weather, that their Governor's *few yards* were just his characteristic way of putting down yards which he well knew were to be counted by hundreds. Then, again, we have the so-called San Fernando Waterworks, an abortion, a scandal for which there is no excuse, as the head of the Public Works Department went his own way despite the experience of those who knew better than he, and the protests of those who would have had to pay. Seventeen Thousand Pounds represent the amount of debt with which Governor Irving's pet department has saddled the town of San Fernando for water, which half the inhabitants cannot get, and which few of the half who do get it dare venture to drink. *Summa fastigia rerum secuti sumus.* If in the works that were so prominent before the public gaze these enormous abuses could flourish, defiant of protest and opposition, what shall we think of the nooks and corners of that same squandering department, which of course must have been mere gnats in the eyes of a Governor who had swallowed so many monstrous camels! The Governor was callous. Trinidad was a battening ground for his friends; but she had in her bosom men who were *her* friends, and the struggle began, constitutionally of course, which, under the leadership of the Mayor of San Fernando, has continued up to now, culminating at last in the Reform movement which Mr. Froude decries, and which his pupil, Mr. S. H. Gatty, is, from what has appeared in the Trinidad papers, doing his "level best" to render abortive.

Sir Sanford Freeling, by the will and pleasure of Downing Street, was the next successor, after Governor Irving, to the chief ruler-ship of Trinidad. Incredible as it may sound, he was a yet more disadvantageous bargain for the Colony's £4000 a year. A better man in many respects than his predecessor, he was in many more a much worse Governor. The personal affability of a man can be known only to those who come into actual contact with him —the public measures of a ruler over a community touches it, mediately or immediately, throughout all its sections. The bad boldness of

Governor Irving achieved much that the people, especially in the outlying districts, could see and appreciate. For example, he erected Rest-houses all over the remoter and more sparsely peopled quarters of the Colony, after the manner of such provisions in Oriental lands. The population who came in contact with these conveniences, and to whom access to them—for a consideration—had never been denied, saw with their own eyes tangible evidence of the Governor's activity, and inferred therefrom a solicitude on his part for the public welfare. Had they, however, been given a notion of the bill which had had to be paid for those frail, though welcome hostelries, they would have stood aghast at the imbecility, or, if not logically that, the something very much worse, through which five times the actual worth of these buildings had been extracted from the Treasury. Sir Sanford Freeling, on the other hand, while being no screener of jobbery and peculation, had not the strength of mind whereof jobbers and peculators do stand in dread. In evidence of that poor ruler's infirmity of purpose, we would only cite the double fact that, whereas in 1883 he was the first to enter a practical protest against the hous-

ing of the diseased and destitute in the then
newly finished, but most leaky, House of Refuge
on the St. Clair Lands, by having the poor
saturated inmates carried off in his presence
to the Colonial Hospital, yet His Excellency
was the very man who, in the very next year,
1884, not only sanctioned the shooting down
of Indian immigrants at their festival, but
actually directed the use of buck-shot for that
purpose! Evidently, if these two foregoing
statements are true, Mr. Froude must join us
in thinking that a man whose mind could be
warped by external influences from the softest
commiseration for the sufferings of his kind,
one year, into being the cold-blooded deviser
of the readiest method for slaughtering unarmed
holiday-makers, the very next year, is not the
kind of ruler whom he and we so cordially de-
siderate.   We have already mentioned above
how ignominious Governor Freeling's failure
was in attempting to meddle with the colossal
abuses of the Public Works Department.

Sir Arthur Elibank Havelock next had the
privilege of enjoying the paradisaic sojourn at
Queen's House, St. Ann's, as well as the
four thousand pounds a year attached to the

right of occupying that princely residence. Save
as a dandy, however, and the harrier of subordinate officials, the writer of the annals of
Trinidad may well pass him by. So then it may
be seen what, by mere freaks of Chance—the
ruling deity at Downing Street—the administrative experience of Trinidad had been from
the departure of that true king in Israel, Sir
Arthur Gordon, up to the visit of Mr. Froude.
First, a slave to red-tape, procrastination, and
the caprices of pretentious colonialists ; next, a
daring schemer, confident of the support of the
then dominant Sugar Interest, and regarding
and treating the resources of the Island as
free booty for his friends, sycophants, and
favourites ; then, an old woman, garbed in
male attire, having an infirmity of purpose
only too prone to be blown about by every wind
of doctrine, alternating helplessly between tenderness and truculence, the charity of a Fry
and the tragic atrocity of Medea. After this
dismal ruler, Trinidad, by the grace of the
Colonial Office, was subjected to the manipulation of an unctuous dandy. This successor of
Gordon, of Elliot, and of Cairns, durst not
oppose high-placed official malfeasants, but

was inexorable with regard to minor delin-
quents. In the above retrospect we have
purposely omitted mentioning such transient
rulers as Mr. Rennie, Sir G. W. Des Vœux,
and last, but by no means least, Sir F. Barlee,
a high-minded Governor, whom death so suddenly and inscrutably snatched away from the
good work he had loyally begun. Every one
of the above temporary administrators was
a right good man for a post in which brain-
power and moral back-bone are essential qualifications. But the Fates so willed it that
Trinidad should never enjoy the permanent
governance of either. In view of the above
facts; in view also of the lessons taught the
inhabitants of Trinadad so frequently, so
cruelly, what wonder is there that, failing of
faith in a probability, which stands one against
four, of their getting another worthy ruler
when Governor Robinson shall have left them,
they should seek to make hay while the sun
shines, by providing against the contingency of
such Governors as they know from bitter experience that Downing Street would place over
their destinies, should the considerations detailed by Mr. Froude or any other equally

unworthy counsellor supervene? That the leading minds of Trinidad should believe in an elective legislature is a logical consequence of the teachings of the past, when the Colony was under the manipulation of the sort of Governors above mentioned as immediately succeeding Sir Arthur Gordon.

This brings us to the motives, the sordid motives, which Mr. Froude, oblivious of the responsibility of his high literary status, has permitted himself gratuitously, and we may add scandalously, to impute to the heads of the Reform movement in Trinidad. It was perfectly competent that our author should decline, as he did decline, to have anything to do, even as a spectator, at a meeting with the object of which he had no sympathy. But our opinion is equally decided that Mr. Froude has transgressed the bounds of decent political antagonism, nay, even of common sense, when he presumes to state that it was not for any other object than the large salaries of the Crown appointments, which they covet for themselves, that the Reform leaders are contending. This is not criticism: it is slander. To make culpatory statements against others, without ability to prove them, is, to say the least, hazardous ; but to make accusations to formulate which the accuser is forced, not only to ignore facts, but actually to deny them, is, to our mind, nothing short of rank defamation.

Mr. Froude is not likely to impress the world (of the West Indies, at any rate) with the transparently silly, if not intentionally malicious, ravings which he has indulged in on the subject of Trinidad and its politics. Here are some of the things which this "champion of Anglo-West Indians" attempts to force down the throats of his readers. He would have us believe that Mr. Francis Damian, the Mayor of Port of Spain, and one of the wealthiest of the native inhabitants of Trinidad, a man who has retired from an honourable and lucrative legal practice, and devotes his time, his talents, and his money to the service of his native country ; that Mr. Robert Guppy, the venerable and venerated Mayor of San Fernando, with his weight of years and his sufficing competence, and with his long record of self-denying services to the public ; that Mr. George Goodwille, one of the most successful merchants in the Colonies ; that Mr. Conrad

F. Stollmeyer, a gentleman retired, in the evening of his days, on his well-earned ample means, are open to the above sordid accusation. In short, that those and such-like individuals who, on account of their private resources and mental capabilities, as well as the public influence resulting therefrom, are, by the sheer logic of circumstances, forced to be at the head of public movements, are actuated by a craving for the few hundred pounds a year for which there is such a scramble at Downing Street among the future official grandees of the West Indies! But granting that this allegation of Mr. Froude's was not as baseless as we have shown it to be, and that the leaders of the Reform agitation were impelled by the desire which our author seeks to discredit them with, what then? Have they who have borne the heat and the burden of the day in making the Colonies what they are no right to the enjoyment of the fruits of their labours? The local knowledge, the confidence and respect of the population, which such men enjoy, and can wield for good or evil in the community, are these matters of small account in the efficient government of the Colony? Our author, in specifying the immunities of his ideal Governor, who is also ours, recommends, amongst other things, that His Excellency should be allowed to choose his own advisers. By this Mr. Froude certainly does not mean that the advisers so chosen must be all pure-blooded Englishmen who have rushed from the destitution of home to batten on the cheaply obtained flesh-pots of the Colonies.

At any rate, whatever political fate Mr. Froude may desire for the Colonies in general, and for Trinidad in particular, it is nevertheless unquestionable that he and the scheme that he may have for our future governance, in this year of grace 1888, have both come into view entirely out of season. The spirit of the times has rendered impossible any further toleration of the arrogance which is based on historical self-glorification. The gentlemen of Trinidad, who are struggling for political enfranchisement, are not likely to heed, except as a matter for indignant contempt, the obtrusion by our author of his opinion that " they had best let well alone." On his own showing, the persons appointed to supreme authority in the Colonies are, more usually than not, entirely unfit for

holding any responsible position whatever over
their fellows. Now, can it be doubted that less
care, less scruple, less consideration, would be
exercised in the choice of the satellites appointed
to revolve, in these far-off latitudes, around the
central luminaries? Have we not found, are
we not still finding every day, that the brain-
dizzinesss — Xenophon calls it κεφαλαλγεια—
induced by sudden promotion has transformed
the abject suppliants at the Downing Street
backstairs into the arrogant defiers of the
opinions, and violators of the rights, of the
populations whose subjection to the British
Crown alone could have rendered possible the
elevation of such folk and their impunity in
malfeasance? The cup of loyal forbearance
reached the overflowing point since the trick-
stering days of Governor Irving, and it is
useless now to believe in the possibility of a
return of the leading minds of Trinidad to
a tame acquiescence as regards the probabilities
of their government according to the Crown
system. Mr. Froude's own remarks point out
definitely enough that a community so governed
is absolutely at the mercy, for good or for evil,
of the man who happens to be invested with

the supreme authority. He has also shown
that in our case that supreme authority is
very often disastrously entrusted. Yet has he
nothing but sneers for the efforts of those who
strive to be emancipated from liability to such
subjection. Mr. Froude's deftly-worded sar-
casms about " degrading tyranny," " the dignity
of manhood," &c., are powerless to alter the
facts. Crown Colony Government—denying, as
it does, to even the wisest and most interested
in a community cursed with it all participation
in the conduct of their own affairs, while in-
vesting irresponsible and uninterested "birds of
passage " (as our author aptly describes them)
with the right of making ducks and drakes of
the resources wrung from the inhabitants—*is*
a degrading tyranny, which the sneers of Mr.
Froude cannot make otherwise. The dignity
of manhood, on the other hand, we are forced
to admit, runs scanty chance of recognition by
any being, however masculine his name, who
could perpetrate such a literary and moral
scandal as "The Bow of Ulysses." Yet the
dignity of manhood stands venerable there,
and whilst the world lasts shall gain for its
possessors the right of record on the roll of

those whom the worthy of the world delight to honour.

All of a piece, as regards veracity and prudence, is the further allegation of Mr. Froude's, to the effect that there was never any agitation for Reform in Trinidad before that which he passes under review. It is, however, a melancholy fact, which we are ashamed to state, that Mr. Froude has written characteristically here also, either through crass ignorance or through deliberate malice. Any respectable, well-informed inhabitant of Trinidad, who happened not to be an official "bird of passage," might, on our author's honest inquiry, have informed him that Trinidad is the land of chronic agitation for Reform. Mr. Froude might also have been informed that, even forty-five years ago, that is in 1843, an elective constitution, with all the electoral districts duly marked out, was formulated and transmitted by the leading inhabitants of Trinidad to the then Secretary of State for the Colonies. He might also have learnt that on every occasion that any of the shady Governors, whom he has so well depicted, manifested any excess of his undesirable qualities, there has been a movement among the educated people in behalf of changing their country's political condition.

We close this part of our review by reiterating our conviction that, come what will, the Crown Colony system, as at present managed, is doomed. Britain may, in deference to the alleged wishes of her impalpable " Anglo-West Indians "—whose existence rests on the authority of Mr. Froude alone—deny to Trinidad and other Colonies even the small modicum prayed for of autonomy, but in doing so the Mother Country will have to sternly revise her present methods of selecting and appointing Governors. As to the subordinate lot, they will have to be worth their salt when there is at the head of the Government a man who is truly deserving of his.

# Negro Felicity in the West Indies.

———◦——

WE come now to the ingenious and novel fashion in which Mr. Froude carries out his investigations among the black population, and to his dogmatic conclusions concerning them. He says :—

"In Trinidad, as everywhere else, my own chief desire was to see the human inhabitants, to learn what they were doing, how they were living, and what they were thinking about, and this could best be done by drives about the town and neighbourhood."

"Drives about the town and neighbourhood," indeed! To learn and be able to depict with faithful accuracy what people "were doing, how they were living, and what they were thinking about"—all this being *best* done (domestic circumstances, nay, soul-workings and all!) through fleeting glimpses of shifting

panoramas of intelligent human beings! What
a bright notion! We have here the suggestion
of a capacity too superhuman to be accepted on
trust, especially when, as in this case, it is by
implication self-arrogated. The modesty of
this thaumaturgic traveller in confining the
execution of his detailed scrutiny of a whole
community to the moderate progression of
some conventional vehicle, drawn by some
conventional quadruped or the other, does
injustice to powers which, if possessed at
all, might have compassed the same achieve-
ment in the swifter transit of an express
train, or, better still perhaps, from the em-
pyrean elevation of a balloon! Yet is Mr.
Froude confident that data professed to be
thus collected would easily pass muster with
the readers of his book! A confidence of this
kind is abnormal, and illustrates, we think
most fully, all the special characteristics of the
man. With his passion for repeating, our
author tells us in continuation of a strange
rhapsody on Negro felicity:—

" Once more, the earth does not contain any
peasantry so well off, so well-cared for, so
happy, so sleek and contented, as the sons

and daughters of the emancipated slaves in the English West Indian Islands."

Again :—

" Under the rule of England, in these islands, the two millions of these brothers-in-law of ours are the most perfectly contented specimens of the human race to be found upon the planet. . . . If happiness be the satisfaction of every conscious desire, theirs is a condition that admits of no improvement : were they independent, they might quarrel among themselves, and the weaker become the bondsmen of the stronger ; under the beneficent despotism of the English Government, which knows no difference of colour and permits no oppression, they can sleep, lounge, and laugh away their lives as they please, fearing no danger," &c.

Now, then, let us examine for a while this roseate picture of Arcadian blissfulness said to be enjoyed by British West Indian Negroes in general, and by the Negroes of Trinidad in particular. " No distinction of colour" under the British rule, and, better still, absolute protection of the weaker against the stronger ! This latter consummation especially,

Mr. Froude tells us, has been happily secured
"under the beneficent despotism" of the
Crown Colony system. However, let the
above vague hyperboles be submitted to the
test of practical experience, and the abstract
government analysed in its concrete relations
with the people.

Unquestionably the actual and direct interposition of the shielding authority above
referred to, between man and man, is the
immediate province of the MAGISTRACY. All
other branches of the Government, having in
themselves no coercive power, must, from the
supreme executive downwards, in cases of
irreconcilable clashing of interests, have ultimate recourse to the magisterial jurisdiction.
Putting aside, then, whatever culpable remiss-
ness may have been manifested by magistrates
in favour of powerful malfeasants, we would
submit that the fact of stipendiary justices
converting the tremendous, far-reaching powers
which they wield into an engine of systematic
oppression, ought to dim by many a shade
the glowing lustre of Mr. Froude's encomiums.
Facts, authentic and notorious, might be adduced in hundreds, especially with respect to

the Port of Spain and San Fernando magis-
stracies (both of which, since the administration
of Sir J. R. Longden, have been exclusively
the prizes of briefless English barristers [1]), to
prove that these gentry, far from being bul-
warks to the weaker as against the stronger,
have, in their own persons, been the direst
scourges that the poor, particularly when
coloured, have been afflicted by in aggravation
of the difficulties of their lot.  Only typical
examples can here be given out of hundreds
upon hundreds which might easily be cited and
proved against the incumbents of the above-
mentioned chief stipendiary magistracies.  One
such example was a matter of everyday discussion at the time of Mr. Froude's visit.  The
inhabitants were even backed in their com-
plaints by the Governor, who had, in response
to their cry of distress, forwarded their prayer

[1] A West Indian official superstition professes to believe
that a British barrister must make an exceptionally good
colonial S.J.P., seeing that he is ignorant of everything, save
general English law, that would qualify him for the post!
In this, to acquit oneself tolerably, some acquaintance
with the language, customs, and habits of thought of the
population is everywhere else held to be of prime importance,
—native conscientiousness and honesty of purpose being
definitively presupposed.

to the home authorities for relief from the hard treatment which they alleged themselves to be suffering at the hands of the then magistrate. Our allusion here is to the chief town, Port of Spain, the magistracy of which embraces also the surrounding districts, containing a total population of between 60,000 and 70,000 souls. Mr. R. D. Mayne filled this responsible office during the latter years of Sir J. R. Longden's governorship. He was reputed, soon after his arrival, to have announced from the bench that in every case he would take the word of a constable in preference to the testimony of any one else. The Barbadian rowdies who then formed the major part of the constabulary of Trinidad, and whose bitter hatred of the older residents had been not only plainly expressed, but often brutally exemplified, rejoiced in the opportunity thus afforded for giving effect to their truculent sentiments. At that time the bulk of the immigrants from Barbados were habitual offenders whom the Government there had provided with a free passage to wherever they elected to betake themselves. The more intelligent of the men flocked to the Trinidad

police ranks, into which they were admitted
generally without much inquiry into their ante-
cedents. On this account they were shunned
by the decent inhabitants, a course which they
repaid with savage animosity. Perjuries the
most atrocious and crushing, especially to the
respectable poor, became the order of the day.
Hundreds of innocent persons were committed
to gaol and the infamy of convict servitude, without the possibility of escape from, or even mitiga-
tion of, their ignominious doom. A respectable
woman (a native of Barbados, too, who in the
time of the first immigration of the better sort
of her compatriots had made Trinidad her
home) was one of the first victims of this
iniquitous state of affairs.

The class of people to which she belonged
was noted as orderly, industrious and law-
abiding, and, being so, it had identified itself
entirely with the natives of the land of its
adoption. This fact alone was sufficient to
involve these immigrants in the same lot of
persecution which their newly arrived countrymen had organized and were carrying out
against the Trinidadians proper. It happened
that, on the occasion to which we wish par-

ticularly to refer, the woman in question was at home, engaged in her usual occupation of ironing for her honest livelihood. Suddenly she heard a heavy blow in the street before her door, and almost simultaneously a loud scream, which, on looking hastily out, she perceived to be the cry of a boy of some ten or twelve years of age, who had been violently struck with the fist by another youth of larger size and evidently his senior in age. The smaller fellow had laid fast hold of his antagonist by the collar, and would not let go, despite the blows which, to extricate himself and in retaliation of the puny buffets of his youthful detainer, he "showered thick as wintry rain."

The woman, seeing the posture of affairs, shouted to the combatants to desist, but to no purpose, rage and absorption in their wrathful occupation having deafened both to all external sounds. Seized with pity for the younger lad, who was getting so mercilessly the worst of it, the woman, hastily throwing a shawl over her shoulders, sprang into the street and rushed between the juvenile belligerents. Dexterously extricating the hand of the little fellow from the collar of his antagonist, she hurried the former into her gateway, shouting out to him at the same time to fasten the door on the inside. This the little fellow did, and no doubt gladly, as this surcease from actual conflict, short though it was, must have afforded space for the natural instinct of self-preservation to reassert itself. Hereupon the elder of the two lads, like a tiger robbed of his prey, sprang furiously to the gate, and began to use frantic efforts to force an entrance. Perceiving this, the woman (who meanwhile had not been idle with earnest dissuasions and remonstrances, which had all proved futile) pulled the irate youngster back, and interposed her body between him and the gate, warding him off with her hands every time that he rushed forward to renew the assault. At length a Barbadian policeman hove in sight, and was hastily beckoned to by the poor ironer, who, by this time, had nearly come to the end of her strength. The uniformed " Bim" was soon on the spot; but, without asking or waiting to hear the cause of the disturbance, he shouted to the volunteer peacemaker, "I see you are fighting: you are my prisoner!" Saying this, he clutched the poor thunderstruck creature by the wrist, and there

and then set about hurrying her off towards
the police station. It happened, however, that
the whole affair had occurred in the sight
of a gentleman of well-known integrity. He,
seated at a window overlooking the street, had
witnessed the whole squabble, from its beginning in words to its culmination in blows; so,
seeing that the woman was most unjustly
arrested, he went out and explained the circumstances to the guardian of order. But to
no purpose; the poor creature was taken to the
station, accompanied by the gentleman, who
most properly volunteered that neighbourly
turn. There she was charged with "obstruct-
ing the policeman in the lawful execution of
his duty." She was let out on bail, and next
day appeared to answer the charge.

Mr. Mayne, the magistrate, presided. The
constable told his tale without any material
deviation from the truth, probably confident,
from previous experience, that his accusation
was sufficient to secure a conviction. On the
defendant's behalf, the gentleman referred to,
who was well known to the magistrate himself, was called, and he related the facts as we
have above given them. Even Mr. Mayne

could see no proof of the information, and this he confessed in the following qualified judgment :—

" You are indeed very lucky, my good woman, that the constable has failed to prove his case against you ; otherwise you would have been sent to hard labour, as the ordinance provides, without the option of a fine. But as the case stands, you must pay a fine of £2 " ! ! !

Comment on this worse than scandalous decision would be superfluous.

Another typical case, illustrative of the truth of Mr. Froude's boast of the eminent fair-play, nay, even the stout protection, that Negroes, and generally, " the weaker," have been wont to receive from British magistrates, may be related.

An honest, hard-working couple, living in one of the outlying districts, cultivated a plot of ground, upon the produce of which they depended for their livelihood. After a time these worthy folk, on getting to their holding in the morning, used to find exasperating evidence of the plunder overnight of their marketable provisions. Determined to discover the depredator, they concealed them-

selves in the garden late one night, and
awaited the result. By that means they
succeeded in capturing the thief, a female,
who, not suspecting their presence, had entered
the garden, dug out some of the provisions,
and was about to make off with her booty. In
spite of desperate resistance, she was taken to
the police station and there duly charged with
larceny. Meanwhile her son, on hearing of
his mother's incarceration, hastened to find
her in her cell, and, after briefly consulting
with her, he decided on entering a countercharge of assault and battery against both her
captors. Whether or not this bold proceeding
was prompted by the knowledge that the dis-
pensing of justice in the magistrate's court
was a mere game of cross-purposes, a cynical
disregard of common sense and elementary
equity, we cannot say ; but the ultimate result
fully justified this abnormal hardihood of filial
championship.

On the day of the trial, the magistrate
heard the evidence on both sides, the case of
larceny having been gone into first. For her
defence, the accused confined herself to simple
denials of the allegations against her, at the

same time entertaining the court with a lachrymose harangue about her rough treatment at the hands of the accusing parties. Finally, the decision of the magistrate was : that the prisoner be discharged, and the plundered goods restored to her ; and, as to the countercharge, that the husband and wife be imprisoned, the former for three and the latter for two months, with hard labour! When we add that there was, at that time, no Governor or Chief Justice accessible to the poorer and less intelligent classes, as is now the case (Sir Henry T. Irving and Sir Joseph Needham having been respectively superseded by Sir William Robinson and Sir John Gorrie), one can imagine what scope there was for similar exhibitions of the protecting energy of British rule.

As we have already said, during Mr. Froude's sojourn in Trinidad the "sleek, happy, and contented" people, whose condition "admitted of no improvement," were yet groaning in bitter sorrow, nay, in absolute despair, under the crushing weight of such magisterial decisions as those which I have just recorded. Let me add two more typical cases which occurred during Mr. Mayne's tenure of office in the island.

L. B. was a member of one of those brawling sisterhoods that frequently disturbed the peace of the town of Port of Spain. She had a "pal" or intimate chum familiarly known as "Lady," who staunchly stood by her in all the squabbles that occurred with their adversaries. One particular night, the police were called to a street in the east of the town, in consequence of an affray between some women of the sort referred to. Arriving on the spot, they found the fight already over, but a war of words was still proceeding among the late combatants, of whom the aforesaid "Lady" was one of the most conspicuous. A list was duly made out of the parties found so engaged, and it included the name of L. B., who happened not to be there, or even in Port of Spain at all, she having some days before gone into the country to spend a little time with some relatives. The inserting of her name was an inferential mistake on the part of the police, arising from the presence of "Lady" at the brawl, she being well known by them to be the inseparable ally of L. B. on such occasions.

It was not unnatural that in the obscurity they should have concluded that the latter was present with her *altera ego*, when in reality she was not there.

The participants in the brawl were charged at the station, and summonses, including one to L. B., were duly issued. On her return to Port of Spain a day or two after the occurrence, the wrongly incriminated woman received from the landlady her key, along with the magisterial summons that had resulted from the error of the constables. The day of the trial came on, and L. B. stood before Mr. Mayne, strong in her innocence, and supported by the sworn testimony of her landlady as well as of her uncle from the country, with whom and with his family she had been uninterruptedly staying up to one or two days after the occurrence in which she had been thus implicated. The evidence of the old lady, who, like thousands of her advanced age in the Colony, had never even once had occasion to be present in any court of justice, was to the following effect: That the defendant, who was a tenant of hers, had, on a certain morning (naming days before the affray occurred), come up to her door well dressed, and followed by a porter carrying her luggage. L. B., she continued, then handed her the key of the apartment, informing her at the same time that she was going for some days into the country to her relatives, for a change, and requesting also that the witness should on no account deliver the key to any person who should ask for it during her absence. This witness further deposed to receiving the summons from the police, which she placed along with the key for delivery to L. B. on the latter's return home.

The testimony of the uncle was also decisively corroborative of that of the preceding witness, as to the absence from Port of Spain of L. B. during the days embraced in the defence. The *alibi* was therefore unquestionably made out, especially as none of the police witnesses would venture to swear to having actually seen L. B. at the brawl. The magistrate had no alternative but that of acquiescing in the proof of her innocence; so he dismissed the charge against the accused, who stood down from among the rest, radiant with satisfaction. The other defendants were duly

convicted, and sentenced to a term of imprisonment with hard labour. All this was quite
correct ; but here comes matter for consideration with regard to the immaculate dispensation
of justice as vaunted so confidently by Mr.
Froude.

On receiving their sentence the women all
stood down from the dock, to be escorted
to prison, except " Lady," who, by the way,
had preserved a rigid silence, while some of
the other defendants had voluntarily and, it
may be added, generously protested that L. B.
was not present on the occasion of this particular row. " Lady," whether out of affection
or from a less respectable motive, cried out to
the stipendiary justice : " But, sir, it ain't fair.
How is it every time that L. B. and me come
up before you, you either fine or send up the
two of us together, and to-day you are sending
*me* up alone ? " Moved either by the logic or
the pathos of this objurgation, the magistrate,
turning towards L. B., who had lingered after
her narrow escape to watch the issue of the
proceedings, thus addressed her :—" L.B., upon
second thoughts I order you to the same term
of hard labour at the Royal Gaol with the

others." The poor girl, having neither money
nor friends intelligent enough to interfere on
her behalf, had to submit, and she underwent
the whole of this iniquitous sentence.

The last typical case that we shall give
illustrates the singular application by this more
than singular judge of the legal maxim *caveat
emptor*. A free coolie possessed of a donkey
resolved to utilize the animal in carting grass
to the market. He therefore called on another
coolie living at some distance from him, whom
he knew to own two carts, a small donkey-cart
and an ordinary cart for mule or horse. He
proposed the purchase of the smaller cart,
stating his reason for wishing to have it. The
donkey-cart was then shown to the intending
purchaser, who, along with two Creole witnesses
brought by him to make out and attest the
receipt on the occasion, found some of the iron
fittings defective, and drew the vendor's attention thereto. He, on his side, engaged, on receiving the amount agreed to for the cart, to
send it off to the blacksmith for immediate
repairs, to be delivered to the purchaser next
morning at the latest. On this understanding
the purchase money was paid down, and the

receipt, specifying that the sum therein mentioned was for a donkey-cart, passed from the
vendor to the purchaser of the little vehicle.
Next day at about noon the man went with
his donkey for the cart. Arrived there, his
countryman had the larger of the two carts
brought out, and in pretended innocence said
to the purchaser of the donkey-cart, "Here
is your cart." On this a warm dispute arose,
which was not abated by the presence and
protests of the two witnesses of the day before,
who had hastily been summoned by the victim
to bear out his contention that it was the
donkey-cart and not the larger cart which had
been examined, bargained for, purchased, and
promised to be delivered, the day before.

The matter, on account of the sturdiness
of the rascal's denials, had to be referred to
a court of law. The complainant engaged ar
able solicitor, who laid the case before Mr.
Mayne in all its transparent simplicity and
strength. The defendant, although he had,
and as a matter of fact could have, no means of
invalidating the evidence of the two witnesses,
and above all of his receipt with his signature,
relied upon the fact that the cart which he

offered was much larger than the one the complainant had actually bought, and that therefore
complainant would be the gainer by the transaction. Incredible as it may sound, this view
of the case commended itself to the magistrate,
who adopted it in giving his judgment against
the complainant. In vain did the solicitor
protest that all the facts of the case were
centred in the desire and intention of the
prosecutor to have specifically a donkey-cart,
which was abundantly proved by everything
that had come out in the proceedings. In vain
also was his endeavour to show that a man
having only a donkey would be hopelessly
embarrassed by having a cart for it which was
entirely intended for animals of much larger
size. The magistrate solemnly reiterated his
decision, and wound up by saying that the
victim had lost his case through disregard of the
legal maxim *caveat emptor*—let the purchaser
be careful. The rascally defendant thus gained
his case, and left the court in defiant triumph.

The four preceding cases are thoroughly
significant of the original method in which
thousands of cases were decided by this model
magistrate, to the great detriment, pecuniary,

social, and moral, during more than ten years, of between 60,000 and 70,000 of the population within the circle of his judicial authority. What shall we think, therefore, of the fairness of Mr. Froude or his informants, who, prompt and eager in imputing unworthy motives to gentlemen with characters above reproach, have yet been so silent with regard to the flagrant and frequent abuses of more than one of their countrymen by whom the honour and fair fame of their nation were for years draggled in the mire, and whose misdeeds were the theme of every tongue and thousands of newspaper-articles in the West Indian Colonies ?

## MR. ARTHUR CHILD, S.J.P.

We now take San Fernando, the next most important magisterial district after Port of Spain. At the time of Mr. Froude's visit, and for some time before, the duties of the magistracy there were discharged by Mr. Arthur Child, an "English barrister" who, of course, had possessed the requisite qualification of being hopelessly briefless. For the ideal justice which Mr. Froude would have Britons believe is meted out to the weaker classes by their fellow-country-

men in the West Indies, we may refer the reader
to the conduct of the above-named functionary
on the memorable occasion of the slaughter of the
coolies under Governor Freeling, in October,
1884. Mr. Child, as Stipendiary Justice, had
the duty of reading the Riot Act to the immigrants, who were marching in procession to the
town of San Fernando, contrary, indeed, to the
Government proclamation which had forbidden
it ; and he it was who gave the order to " fire,"
which resulted fatally to many of the unfortunate devotees of Hosein. This mandate and its
lethal consequences anticipated by some minutes
the similar but far more death-dealing action
of the Chief of Police, who was stationed at
another post in the vicinity of San Fernando.
The day after the shooting down of a total of
more than one hundred immigrants, the protecting action of this magistrate towards the
weaker folk under his jurisdiction had a striking exemplification, to which Mr. Froude is
hereby made welcome. Of course there was a
general cry of horror throughout the Colony,
and especially in the San Fernando district, at
the fatal outcome of the proclamation, which had
mentioned only " fine " and " imprisonment,"

but not Death, as the penalty of disregarding its prohibitions. For nearly forty years, namely from their very first arrival in the Colony, the East Indian immigrants had, according to specific agreement with the Government, invariably been allowed the privilege of celebrating their annual feast of Hosein, by walking in procession with their pagodas through the public roads and streets of the island, without prohibition or hindrance of any kind from the authorities, save and except in cases where rival estate pagodas were in danger of getting into collision on the question of precedence. On such occasions the police, who always attended the processions, usually gave the lead to the pagodas of the labourers of estates according to their seniority as immigrants.

In no case up to 1884, after thirty odd years' inauguration in the Colony, was the Hosein festival ever pretended to be any cause of danger, actual or prospective, to any town or building. On the contrary, business grew brisker and solidly improved at the approach of the commemoration, owing to the very considerable sale of parti-coloured paper, velvet, calico, and similar articles used in the construc-

tion of the pagodas. Governor Freeling, however, was, it may be presumed, compelled to
see danger in an institution which had had
nearly forty years' trial, without a single accident
happening to warrant any sudden interposition
of the Government tending to its suppression.
At all events, the only action taken in 1884, in
prospect of their usual festival, was to notify the
immigrants by proclamation, and, it is said, also
through authorized agents, that the details of
their fête were not to be conducted in the
usual manner ; and that their appearance with
pagodas in any public road or any town, without special license from some competent local
authority, would entail the penalty of so many
pounds fine, or imprisonment for so many
months with hard labour. The immigrants, to
whom this unexpected change on the part of the
authorities was utterly incomprehensible, both
petitioned and sent deputations to the Governor, offering guarantees for the, if possible,
more secure celebration of the Hosein, and
praying His Excellency to cancel the prohibition as to the use of the roads, inasmuch as it in-
terfered with the essential part of their religious
rite, which was the "drowning," or casting into

the sea, of the pagodas. Having utterly failed
in their efforts with the Governor, the coolies
resolved to carry out their religious duty according to prescriptive forms, accepting, at the
same time, the responsibility in the way of fine
or imprisonment which they would thus inevitably incur. A rumour was also current at
the time that, pursuant to this resolution, the
head men of the various plantations had authorized a general subscription amongst their
countrymen, for meeting the contingency of
fines in the police courts. All these things
were the current talk of the population of San
Fernando, in which town the leading immigrants, free as well as indentured, had begun
to raise funds for this purpose.

All that the public, therefore, expected would
have resulted from the intended infringement
of the Proclamation was an enormous influx
of money in the shape of fines into the
Colonial Treasury ; as no one doubted the
extreme facility which existed for ascertaining
exactly, in the case of persons registered and
indentured to specific plantations, the names
and abodes of at least the chief offenders
against the proclamation. Accordingly, on the

occurrence of the bloody catastrophe related
above, every one felt that the mere persistence
in marching *all unarmed* towards the town,
without actually attempting to force their way
into it, was exorbitantly visited upon the coolies
by a violent death or a life-long mutilation.
This sentiment few were at any pains to
conceal; but as the poorer and more ignorant
classes can be handled with greater impunity
than those who are intelligent and have the
means of self-defence, Mr. Justice Child, the
very day after the tragedy, and without waiting
for the *pro formâ* official inquiry into the
tragedy in which he bore so conspicuous a part,
actually caused to be arrested, sat to try and
sent to hard labour, persons whom the police,
in obedience to his positive injunctions, had
reported to him as having condemned the
shooting down of the immigrants! Those who
were arrested and thus summarily punished
had, of course, no means of self-protection; and
as the case is typical of others, as illustrative of
"justice-made law" applied to "subject races"
in a British colony, Mr. Froude is free to accept
it, or not, in corroboration of his unqualified
panegyrics.

### MR. GROVE HUMPHREY CHAPMAN, S.J.P.

As Stipendary Magistrate of this self-same San Fernando district, Grove Humphrey Chapman, Esquire (another English barrister), was the immediate predecessor of Mr. Child. More humane than Mr. Mayne, his colleague and contemporary in Port of Spain, this young magistrate began his career fairly well. But he speedily fell a victim to the influences immediately surrounding him in his new position. His head, which later events proved never to have been naturally strong, began to be turned by the unaccustomed deference which he met with on all hands, from high and low, official and non-official, and he himself soon consummated the addling of his brain by persistent practical revolts against every maxim of the ancient Nazarenes in the matter of potations. His decisions at the court, therefore, became perfect emulations of those of Mr. Mayne, as well in perversity as in harshness, and many in his case also were the appeals for relief made to the head of the executive by the inhabitants of the district—but of course in vain. Governor Irving was at this time in office, and the unfortunate

victims of perverse judgments—occasionally
pronounced by this magistrate in his cups—
were only poor Negroes, coolies, or other
persons whose worldly circumstances placed
them in the category of the "weaker" in the
community. To these classes of people that
excellent ruler unhappily denied—we dare not
say his personal sympathy, but—the official
protection which, even through self-respect,
he might have perfunctorily accorded. Bent,
however, on running through the whole gamut
of extravagance, Mr. Chapman—by interpreting
official impunity into implying a direct license
for the wildest of his caprices—plunged head-
long with ever accelerating speed, till the
deliverance of the Naparimas became the
welcome consequence of his own personal
action. On one occasion it was credibly
reported in the Colony that this infatuated
dispenser of British justice actually stretched
his official complaisance so far as to permit a
lady not only to be seated near him on the
judicial bench, but also to take a part—loud,
boisterous and abusive—in the legal proceedings of the day. Meanwhile, as the Governor
could not be induced to interfere, things went

on from bad to worse, till one day, as above
hinted, the unfortunate magistrate so publicly
committed himself as to be obliged to be
borne for temporary refuge to the Lunatic
Asylum, whence he was clandestinely shipped
from the Colony on "six months' leave of
absence," never more to resume his official
station.

The removal of two such magistrates
as those whose careers we have so briefly
sketched out—Mr. Mayne having died, still
a magistrate, since Mr. Froude's departure
—has afforded opportunity for the restoration
of British protecting influence. In the person
of Mr. Llewellyn Lewis, as magistrate of
Port of Spain, this opportunity has been
secured. He, it is generally rumoured, strives
to justify the expectations of fair play and even-
handed justice which are generally entertained
concerning Englishmen. It is, however, certain
that with a Governor so prompt to hear the cry
of the poor as Sir William Robinson has proved
himself to be, and with a Chief Justice so
vigilant, fearless, and painstaking as Sir John
Gorrie, the entire magistracy of the Colony
must be so beneficially influenced as to preclude

the frequency of appeals being made to the higher courts, or it may be to the Executive, on account of scandalously unjust and senseless decisions.

So long, too, as the names of T. S. Warner, Captain Larcom, and F. H. Hamblin abide in the grateful remembrance of the entire population, as ideally upright, just, and impartial dispensers of justice, each in his own jurisdiction, we can only sigh at the temporal dispensation which renders practicable the appointment and retention in office of such administrators of the Law as were Mr. Mayne and Mr. Chapman. The widespread and irreparable mischiefs wrought by these men still affect disastrously many an unfortunate household ; and the execration by the weaker in the community of their memory, particularly that of Robert Dawson Mayne, is only a fitting retribution for their abuse of power.

BOOK III.

# Social Revolution.

———◦◦———

Never was the Knight of La Mancha more convinced of his imaginary mission to redress the wrongs of the world than Mr. James Anthony Froude seems to be of his ability to alter the course of events, especially those bearing on the destinies of the Negro in the British West Indies. The doctrinaire style of his utterances, his sublime indifference as to what Negro opinion and feelings may be, on account of his revelations, are uniquely charming. In that portion of his book headed "Social Revolution" our author, with that mixture of frankness and cynicism which is so dear to the soul of the British *esprit fort* of to-day, has challenged a comparison between British Colonial policy on the

8

one hand, and the Colonial policy of France
and Spain on the other. This he does with an
evident recklessness that his approval of Spain
and France involves a definite condemnation
of his own country. However, let us hear
him :—

"The English West Indies, like other parts
of the world, are going through a silent revolution. Elsewhere the revolution, as we hope, is
a transition state, a new birth ; a passing away
of what is old and worn out, that a fresh and
healthier order may rise in its place. In the
West Indies the most sanguine of mortals
will find it difficult to entertain any such *hope
at all.*"

As Mr. Froude is speaking dogmatically
here of *his*, or rather *our*, West Indies, let
us hear him as he proceeds :—

"We have been a ruling power there for two
hundred and fifty years ; the *whites whom we
planted as our representatives* are drifting into
ruin, and they regard England and England's
policy as the principal cause of it. The *blacks
whom, in a fit of virtuous benevolence*, we emancipated, do not feel *particularly obliged to us.*
They think, if they think at all, that they were

ill-treated originally, and have received no more than was due to them."

Thus far. Now, as to " the *whites* whom we planted as our *representatives,*" and who, Mr. Froude avers, are drifting into ruin, we confess to a total ignorance of their whereabouts in these islands in this jubilee year of Negro Emancipation. Of the *representatives* of Britain immediately before and after Emancipation we happen to know something, which, on the testimony of Englishmen, Mr. Froude will be made quite welcome to before our task is ended. With respect to Mr. Froude's statement as to the ingratitude of the emancipated Blacks, if it is aimed at the slaves who were actually set free, it is utterly untrue; for no class of persons, in their humble and artless way, are more attached to the Queen's majesty, whom they regard as incarnating in her gracious person the benevolence which Mr. Froude so jauntily scoffs at. But if our censor's remark under this head is intended for the present generation of Blacks, it is a pure and simple absurdity. What are *we* Negroes of the present day to be grateful for to the us, personified by Mr. Froude and the Colonial

Office exportations ?   We really believe, from
what we know of Englishmen, that very
few indeed would regard Mr. Froude's reproach otherwise than as a palpable adding
of insult to injury.   Obliged to "us," indeed !
Why, Mr. Froude, who speaks of us as dogs
and horses, suggests that the same kindliness
of treatment that secures the attachment of
those noble brutes would have the same result
in our case.   With the same consistency that
marks his utterances throughout his book, he
tells his readers "that there is no original or
congenital difference between the capacity of
the White and the Negro races." He adds, too,
significantly : "With the *same chances* and with
the same *treatment*, I believe that distinguished
men would be produced *equally* from *both*
races."   After this truthful testimony, which
Pelion upon Ossa of evidence has confirmed,
does Mr. Froude, in the fatuity of his skin-
pride, believe that educated men, worthy of the
name, would be otherwise than resentful, if not
disgusted, at being shunted out of bread in
their own native land, which their parents'
labours and taxes have made desirable, in
order to afford room to blockheads, vulgarians,

or worse, imported from beyond the seas? Does Mr. Froude's scorn of the Negroes' skin extend, inconsistently on his part, to their intelligence and feelings also? And if so, what has the Negro to care — if let alone and not wantonly thwarted in his aspirations? It sounds queer, not to say unnatural and scandalous, that Englishmen should in these days of light be the champions of injustice towards their fellow-subjects, not for any intellectual or moral disqualification, but on the simple account of the darker skin of those who are to be assailed and thwarted in their life's career and aspirations. Really, are we to be grateful that the colour difference should be made the basis and justification of the dastardly denials of justice, social, intellectual, and moral, which have characterized the *régime* of those who Mr. Froude boasts were left to be the representatives of Britain's morality and fair play? Are the Negroes under the French flag not intensely French? Are the Negroes under the Spanish flag not intensely Spanish? Wherefore are they so? It is because the French and Spanish nations, who are neither of them inferior in origin or the

nobility of the part they have each played
on the historic stage, have had the dignity
and sense to understand the lowness of moral
and intellectual consciousness implied in the
subordination of questions of an imperial
nature to the slaveholder's anxiety about the
hue of those who are to be benefited or not
in the long run.   By Spain and France every
loyal and law-abiding subject of the Mother
Country has been a citizen deemed worthy all
the rights, immunities, and privileges flowing
from good and creditable citizenship.   Those
meriting such distinction were taken into the
bosom of the society which their qualifications
recommended them to share, and no office
under the Government has been thought too
good or too elevated for men of their stamp.
No wonder, then, that Mr. Froude is silent
regarding the scores of brilliant coloured
officials who adorn the civil service of France
and Spain, and whose appointment, in contrast
with what has usually been the case in British
Colonies, reflects an abiding lustre on those
countries, and establishes their right to a foremost place among nations.

Mr. Froude, in speaking of Chief Justice

Reeves, ventures upon a smart truism which
we can discuss for him, but of course not in the
sense in which he has meant it. "Exceptions,"
our author remarks, "are supposed proverbially
to prove nothing, or to prove the very opposite
of what they appear to prove. When a particular phenomenon occurs rarely, the probabilities are strong against the recurrence of
it." Now, is it in ignorance, or through dis-
ingenuousness, that Mr. Froude has penned
this argument regarding exceptions? Surely,
in the vast area of American life, it is not
possible that he could see Frederick Douglass
*alone* out of the cluster of prominent Black
Americans who are doing the work of their
country so worthily and so well in every official
department. Anyhow, Mr. Froude's history of
the Emancipation may here be amended for
him by a reminder that, in the British Colonies,
it was not *Whites* as masters, and *Blacks* as
slaves, who were affected by that momentous
measure. In fact, 1838 found in the British
Colonies very nearly as many Negro and
Mulatto slave-owners as there were white.
Well then, these black and yellow planters
received their quota, it may be presumed, of

the £20,000,000 sterling indemnity. They
were part and parcel of the proprietary body
in the Colonies, and had to meet the crisis
like the rest. They were very wealthy, some
of these Ethiopic accomplices of the oppressors
of their own race. Their sons and daughters
were sent, like the white planter's children,
across the Atlantic for a European education.
These young folk returned to their various
native Colonies as lawyers and doctors. Many
of them were also wealthy planters. The
daughters, of course, became in time the
mothers of the new generation of prominent
inhabitants. Now, in America all this was different. No " nigger," however alabaster fair,
was ever allowed the privileges of common
citizenship, let alone the right to hold property
in others. If possessed by a weakness to pass
for white men, as very many of them could
easily have contrived to do, woe unto the poor
impostors ! They were hunted down from city
to city as few felons would be, and finally
done to death—"serve them right!" being
the grim commentary regarding their fate for
having sought to usurp the ineffable privilege
of whitemanship ! All this, Mr. Froude, was

the rule, the practice, in America, with regard to persons of colour up to twenty-five years ago. Now, sir, what is the phenomenon which strikes your vision in that mighty Republic to-day, with regard to those self-same despised, discountenanced, persecuted and harried descendants of Ham? We shall tell you of the change that has taken place in their condition, and also some of the reasons of that beneficent revolution.

The Proclamation of Emancipation on January 1st, 1863, was, by President Lincoln, frankly admitted to have been a war necessity. No abstract principle of justice or of morals was of primary consideration in the matter. The saving of the Union at any cost,—that is, the stern political emergency forced forth the document which was to be the social salvation of every descendant of Ham in the United States of America. Close upon the heels of their emancipation, the enfranchisement of the Negroes was pushed forward by the thorough-going American statesmen. They had no sentimentality to defer to. The logic of events— the fact not only of the coloured race being freedmen, but also of their having been effec-

tive comrades on the fields of battle, where the
blood of eager thousands of them had flowed
on the Union side, pointed out too plainly
that men with such claims should also be
partners in the resulting triumph.

Mr. Froude, being so deferential to skin-
prejudice, will doubtless find it strange that
such a measure as the Civil Rights Bill
should have passed a Congress of Americans.
Assuredly with the feeling against the coloured
race which custom and law had engrafted into
the very nature of the vast majority, this
was a tremendous call to make on the national
susceptibilities.  But it has been exactly this
that has brought out into such vivid contrast
the conduct of the British statesman, loudly
professing to be unprejudiced as to colour,
and fair and humane, on the one hand, and, on
the other hand, the dealings of the politicians of
America, who had, as a matter of fact, sucked in
aversion and contempt towards the Negro together with their mother's milk.  Of course no
sane being could expect that feelings so deeply
ingrained and nourished could be rooted out
by logic or by any legislative enactment.
But, indeed, it is sublimely creditable to

the American Government that, whatever
might be the personal and private sentiments
of its individual members as regards race,
*palmam ferat qui meruit*—"let him bear the
palm who has deserved it"—has been their
motto in dealing generally with the claims
of their Ethiopic fellow-citizens.   Hence it is
that in only twenty-five years America can
show Negro public officers as thick as black-
berries, while Mr. Froude can mention only
Mr. Justice Reeves in FIFTY years as a sample
of the "exceptional" progress under British
auspices of a man of African descent!  Verily,
if in fifty long years British policy can recognize only one single exception in a race between which and the white race there is no
original or congenital difference of capacity, the
inference must be that British policy has been
not only systematically, but also too successfully,
hostile to the advancement of the Ethiopians
subject thereto; while the "fair field and no
favour" management of the strong-minded
Americans has, by its results, confirmed the
culpability of the English policy in its relation
to "subject races."

The very suggestive section of " the English

in the West Indies," from which we have already given extracts, and which bears the title " Social Revolution," thus proceeds :—

" But it does not follow that what can be done *eventually* can be done *immediately*, and the gulf which divides the colours is no arbitrary prejudice, but has been opened by the centuries of training and discipline which have given us the start in the race " (p. 125).

The reference in the opening clause of the above citation, as to what is *eventually* possible not being *immediately* feasible, is to the elevation of Blacks to high official posts, such as those occupied by Judge Reeves in Barbados, and by Mr. F. Douglass in the United States. We have already disposed by anticipation of the above contention of Mr. Froude's, by showing that in only twenty-five years America has found *hundreds* of eminent Blacks to fill high posts under her government. Our author's futile mixture of Judge Reeves' exceptional case with that of Fred. Douglass, which he cunningly singles out from among so many in the United States, is nothing but a subterfuge, of the same queer and flimsy description with which the literature of the cause now cham-

pioned by his eloquence has made the world only
too familiar. What can Mr. Froude conceive
any sane man should see in common between
the action of British and of American statesmanship in the matter now under discussion ? If
his utterance on this point is that of a British
spokesman, let him abide by his own verdict
against his own case, as embodied in the words,
" the gulf which divides the two COLOURS is no
arbitrary prejudice," which, coupled with his
contention that the elevation of the Blacks is
not *immediately* feasible, discloses the wideness
of divergence between British and American
political opinion on this identical subject.

Mr. Froude is pathetically eloquent on the
colour question. He tells of the wide gulf
between the two colours—we suppose it is as
wide as exists between his white horse and his
black horse. Seriously, however, does not this
kind of talk savour only too much of the slave-
pen and the auction-block of the rice-swamp
and the cotton-field ; of the sugar-plantation
and the driver's lash ? In the United States
alone, among all the slave-holding Powers, was
the difference of race and colour invoked openly
and boldly to justify all the enormities that

were the natural accompaniments of those " institutions " of the Past. But is Mr. Froude serious in invoking the ostracizing of inno- cent, loyal, and meritorious British subjects on account of their mere colour? Physical slavery—which was no crime *per se*, Mr. Froude tells us—had at least overwhelming brute power, and that silent, passive force which is even more potential as an auxiliary, viz., unen- lightened public opinion, whose neutrality is too often a positive support to the empire of wrong. But has Mr. Froude, in his present wild pro- paganda on behalf of political and, therefore, of social repression, anything analogous to those two above-specified auxiliaries to rely on? We trow not. Then why this frantic bluster and shouting forth of indiscreet aspirations on be- half of a minority to whom accomplished facts, when not agreeable to or manipulated by them- selves, are a perpetual grievance, generating life-long impotent protestations? Presumably there are possibilities the thoughts of which fascinate our author and his congeners in this, to our mind, vain campaign in the cause of social retrogression. But, be the incentives what they may, it might not be amiss on our part to suggest to those impelled by them that the ignoring of Negro opinion in their calculations, though not only possible but easily practised fifty years ago, is a portentous blunder at the present time. *Verbum sapienti.*

Mr. Froude must see that he has set about his Negro-repression campaign in too blundering a fashion. He evidently expects to be able to throw dust into the eyes of the intelligent world, juggler-wise, through the agency of the mighty pronoun US, as representing the entire Anglo-Saxon race, in his advocacy of the now scarcely intelligible pretensions of a little coterie of Her Majesty's subjects in the West Indies. These gentry are hostile, he urges, to the presence of progressive Negroes on the soil of the tropics ! Yet are these self-same Negroes not only natives, but active improvers and embellishers of that very soil. We cannot help concluding that this impotent grudge has sprung out of the additional fact that these identical Negroes constitute also a living refutation of the sinister predictions ventured upon generally against their race, with frantic recklessness, even within the last three decades, by affrighted slave-holders, of whose ravings Mr. Froude's book is only a diluted echo, out of season and outrageous to the conscience of modern civilization.

It is patent, then, that the matters which Mr. Froude has sought to force up to the dignity of genetic rivalship, has nothing of that importance about it.    His US, between whom and the Negro subjects of Great Britain the gulf of colour lies, comprises, as he himself owns, an outnumbered and, as we hope to prove later on, a not over-creditable little clique of Anglo-Saxon lineage.    The real US who have started ahead of the Negroes, " through the training and discipline of centuries," are assuredly *not* anything like " represented " by the few pretentious incapables who, instead of conquering predominance, as they who deserve it always do, like men, are whimpering like babies after dearly coveted but utterly unattainable enjoyments—to be had at the expense of the interests of the Negroes whom they, rather amusingly, affect to despise.    When Mr. Froude shall have become able to present for the world's contemplation a question respecting which the Anglo-Saxon family, in its grand world-wide predominance, and the African family, in its yet feeble, albeit promising, incipience of self-adjustment, shall actually be competitors, then, and only then, will it be time to accept the outlook as serious. But when, as in the present case, he invokes the whole prestige of the Anglo-Saxon race in favour of the untenable pretensions of a few *blasés* of that race, and that to the social and political detriment of tens of thousands of black fellow-subjects, it is high time that the common sense of civilization should laugh him out of court. The US who are flourishing, or pining, as the case may be, in the British West Indies —by favour of the Colonial Office on the former hypothesis, or, on the second, through the mis-direction of their own faculties—do not, and, in the very nature of things, cannot in any race take the lead of any set of men endowed with virile attributes, the conditions of the contest being on all sides identical.

Pass we onward to extract and comment on other passages in this very engaging section of Mr. Froude's book. On the same page (125) he says :—

" The African Blacks have been free enough for thousands, perhaps for ten thousands of years, and it has been the absence of restraint which has prevented them from becoming civilized."

All this, perhaps, is quite true, and, in the absence of positive evidence to the contrary of our author's dogmatic assertions, we save time by allowing him all the benefit he can derive from whatever weight they might carry.

"Generation has followed generation, and the children are as like their fathers as the successive generations of apes."

To this we can have nothing to object ; especially in view of what the writer goes on to say, and that on his own side of the hedge— somewhat qualified though his admission may be :—" The whites, *it is likely enough*, succeeded one another with the same similarity for a series of ages." Our speculator grows profoundly philosophic here ; and in this mood thus entertains his readers in a strain which, though deep, we shall strive to find clear :—

" It is now supposed that human race has been on the planet for a hundred thousand years at least ; and the first traces of civilization cannot be thrown back at furthest beyond six thousand. During all this time mankind went on treading in the same steps, century after century making no more advance than the birds and beasts."

In all this there is nothing that can usefully be taken exception to ; for speculation and conjecture, if plausible and attractive, are free to revel whenever written documents and the unmistakable indications of the earth's crust are both entirely at fault. Warming up with his theme, Mr. Froude gets somewhat ambiguous in the very next sentence. Says he :—

"In Egypt or India or one knows not where, *accident or natural development* quickened into life our moral and intellectual faculties ; and these faculties have grown into what we now experience, not in the freedom in which the modern takes delight, but under the sharp rule of the strong over the weak, of the wise over the unwise."

Our author, as we see, begins his above quoted deliverance quite at a loss with regard to the agency to which the incipience, growth, and fructification of man's faculties should be attributed. "Accident," "natural development," he suggests, quickened the human faculties into the progressive achievements which they have accomplished. But then, wherefore is this writer so forcible, so confident in his prophecies regarding Negroes and their future temporal condition and proceedings, since it is "accident," and " accident" only, that must determine their fulfilment ? Has he so securely bound the fickle divinity to his service as to be certain of its agency in the realization of his forecasts ?   And if so, where then would be the *fortuitousness* that is the very essence of occurrences that glide, undesigned, unexpected, unforeseen, into the domain of Fact, and become material for History ?   So far as we feel capable of intelligently meditating on questions of this inscrutable nature, we are forced to conclude that since "natural development" could be so regular, so continuous, and withal so efficient, in the production of the marvellous results that we daily contemplate, there must be existent and in operation—as, for instance, in the case of the uniformity characterizing for ages successive generations of mankind, as above adduced by our philosopher himself—some controlling LAW, according and subject to which no check has marred the harmonious progression, or prevented the consummations that have crowned the normal exercise of human energy, intellectual as well as physical.

"The *sharp* rule of the *strong* over the

*weak,*" is the first clause of the Carlylean-
sounding phrase which embodies the requisite
conditions for satisfactory human development.
The terms expressive of these conditions, however, while certainly suggesting and embracing
the beneficent, elevating influence and discipline
of European civilization, such as we know and
appreciate it, do not by any means exclude the
domination of Mr. Legree or any other typical
man-monster, whose power over his fellow-
creatures is at once a calamity to the victims
and a disgrace to the community tolerating not
only its exercise, but the very possibility of its
existence. The sharp rule of " the *wise* over
the *unwise,*" is the closing section of the
recommendation to ensure man's effective development. Not even savages hesitate to defer
in all their important designs to the sought-for
guidance of superior judgments. But in the
case of us West Indian Blacks, to whom Mr.
Froude's doctrine here has a special reference,
is it suggested by him that the bidders for predominance over us on the purely epidermal, the
white skin, ground, are *ipso facto* the monopolists
of directing wisdom ? It surely cannot be so ; for
Mr. Froude's own chapters regarding both the

nomination by Downing Street of future Colonial
office-holders and the disorganized mental and
moral condition of the indigenous representatives—as he calls them!—of his country in these
climes, preclude the possibility that the reference
regarding the wise can be to *them.*   Now since
this is so, we really cannot see why the pains
should have been taken to indite the above
truism, to the truth whereof, under every
normal or legitimate circumstance, the veriest
barbarian, by spontaneously resorting to and
cheerfully abiding by it, is among the first to
secure practical effect.

"Our own Anglo-Saxon race," continues our
author, "has been capable of self-government
only after a thousand years of civil and spiritual
authority.   European government, European
instruction, continued steadily till his natural
tendencies are superseded by higher instincts,
may shorten the probation period of the negro.
Individual blacks of exceptional quality, like
Frederick Douglass in America, or the Chief
Justice of Barbados, *will avail themselves* of
opportunities to rise, and the freest opportunity
OUGHT TO BE *offered* them."   Here we are reminded of the dogma laid down by a certain

class of ethnologists, to the effect that intellec-
tuality, when displayed by a person of mixed
European and African blood, must always be
assigned to the European side of the parentage;
and in the foregoing citation our author speaks
of two personages undoubtedly belonging to the
class embraced in the above dogma. Three
specific objections may, therefore, be urged
against the statements which we have indicated
in the above quotation. First and foremost,
neither Judge Reeves nor Mr. Fred Douglass
is a *black man*, as Mr. Froude inaccurately
represents each of them to be. The former is of
mixed blood, to what degree we are not adepts
enough to determine; and the latter, if his
portrait and those who have personally seen
him mislead us not, is a decidedly fair man.

We, of course, do not for a moment imagine
that either of those eminent descendants of
Ham cares a jot about the settlement of this
question, which doubtless would appear very
trivial to both. But as our author's crusade is
against the Negro—by which we understand the
*undiluted* African descendant, the *pure* Negro,
as he singularly describes Chief Justice Reeves
—our anxiety is to show that there exist, both

in the West Indies and in the United States, scores of genuine black men to whom neither of these two distinguished patriots would, for one instant, hesitate to concede any claim to equality in intellectual and social excellence. The second exception which we take is, as we have already shown in a previous page, to the persistent lugging in of America by Mr. Froude, doubtless to keep his political country-men in countenance with regard to the Negro question. We have already pointed out the futility of this proceeding on our author's part, and suggested how damaging it might prove to the cause he is striving to uphold. " Blacks of exceptional quality," like the two gentlemen he has specially mentioned, " will avail themselves of opportunities to rise." Most certainly they *will*, Mr. Froude—but, for the present, only in America, where those opportunities are really free and open to all. There no parasitical non-workers are to be found, eager to eat bread, but in the sweat of other people's brows ; no impecunious title-bearers ; no importunate bores, nor other similar characters whom the Government there would regard it as their duty "to provide for "—by quartering them on the reve-

nues of Colonial dependencies. But in the
British Crown—or rather " Anglo-West Indian "
—governed Colonies, has it ever been, can it
ever be, thus ordered ? Our author's description of the exigencies that compel injustice to
be done in order to requite, or perhaps to secure,
Parliamentary support, coupled with his account
of the bitter animus against the coloured race
that rankles in the bosom of his " Englishmen
in the West Indies," sufficiently proves the utter
hypocrisy of his recommendation, that the *freest*
opportunities should be *offered* to Blacks of the
said exceptional order. The very wording of
Mr. Froude's recommendation is disingenuous.
It is one stone sped at two birds, and which,
most naturally, has missed them both.

Mr. Froude knew perfectly well that, twenty-
five years before he wrote his book, America
had thrown open the way to public advance
ment to the Blacks, as it had been previously
free to Whites alone. His use of " should be
offered," instead of "are offered," betrays his
consciousness that, at the time he was writing,
the offering of any opportunities of the kind
he suggests was a thing still to be desired
under British jurisdiction. The third objec-

tion which we shall take to Mr. Froude's bracket-
ing of the cases of Mr. Fred Douglass and of
Judge Reeves together, is that, when closely
examined, the two cases can be distinctly seen
to be not in any way parallel.   The applause
which our author indirectly bids for on behalf
of British Colonial liberality in the instance of
Mr. Reeves would be the grossest mockery, if
accorded in any sense other than we shall proceed to show.   Fred Douglass was born and
bred a slave in one of the Southern States of
the Union, and regained his freedom by flight
from bondage, a grown man, and, of course,
under the circumstances, solitary and destitute.
He reached the North at a period when the
prejudice of the Whites against men of his race
was so rampant as to constitute a positive
mania.

The stern and cruelly logical doctrine, that a
Negro had no rights which white men were
bound to respect, was in full blast and practical
exemplification.   Yet amidst it all, and despite
of it all, this gifted fugitive conquered his way
into the Temple of Knowledge, and became
eminent as an orator, a writer, and a lecturer
on political and general subjects.   Hailed abroad

as a prodigy, and received with acclamation into
the brotherhood of intelligence, abstract justice
and moral congruity demanded that such a man
should no longer be subject to the shame and
abasement of social, legal, and political proscription. The land of his birth proved herself
equal to this imperative call of civilized Duty,
regardless of customs and the laws, written as
well as unwritten, which had doomed to life-long
degradation every member of the progeny of
Ham. Recognizing in the erewhile bondman
a born leader of men, America, with the un-
flinching directness that has marked her course,
whether in good or in evil, responded with
spontaneous loyalty to the inspiration of her
highest instincts. Shamed into compunction
and remorse at the solid fame and general
sympathy secured for himself by a son of her
soil, whom, in the wantonness of pride and
power, she had denied all fostering care (not,
indeed, for any conscious offending on his part,
but by reason of a natural peculiarity which she
had decreed penal), America, like a repentant
mother, stooped from her august seat, and
giving with enthusiasm both hands to the out-
cast, she helped him to stand forward and erect,

in the dignity of untrammeled manhood, making him, at the same time, welcome to a place of honour amongst the most gifted, the worthiest and most favoured of her children.

Chief Justice Reeves, on the other hand, did not enter the world, as Douglass had done, heir to a lot of intellectual darkness and legalized social and political proscription. Associated from adolescence with S. J. Prescod, the greatest leader of popular opinion whom Barbados has yet produced, Mr. Reeves possessed in his nature the material to assimilate and reflect in his own principles and conduct the salient characteristics of his distinguished Mentor. Arrived in England to study law, he had there the privilege of the personal acquaintance of Lord Brougham, then one of the Nestors of the great Emancipation conflict. On returning to his native island, which he did immediately after his call to the bar, Mr. Reeves sprung at once into the foremost place, and retained his precedence till his labours and aspirations were crowned by his obtaining the highest judicial post in that Colony. For long years before becoming Chief Justice, Mr. Reeves had conquered for himself the respect and confidence of all Barbadians—even including the ultra exclusive " Anglo-West-Indians " of Mr. Froude —by the manful constitutional stand which, sacrificing official place, he had successfully made against the threatened abrogation of the Charter of the Colony, which every class and colour of natives cherish and revere as a most precious, almost sacred, inheritance. The successful champion of their menaced liberties found clustering around him the grateful hearts of all his countrymen, who, in their hour of dread at the danger of their time-honoured constitution, had clung in despair to him as the only leader capable of heading the struggle and leading the people, by wise and constitutional guidance, to the victory which they desired but could not achieve for themselves.

Sir William Robinson, who was sent out as pacificator, saw and took in at a glance the whole significance of the condition of affairs, especially in their relation to Mr. Reeves, and *vice versâ.* With the unrivalled pre-eminence and predominant personal influence of the latter, the Colonial Office had possessed more than ample means of being perfectly familiar. What, then, could be more natural and consonant with sound policy than that the then acknowledged, but officially unattached, head of the people (being an eminent lawyer), should, on the occurrence of a vacancy in the highest juridical post, be appointed to co-operate with the supreme head of the Executive? Mr. Reeves was already the chief of the legal body of the Colony; his appointment, therefore, as Chief Justice amounted to nothing more than an official ratification of an accomplished and unalterable fact. Of course, it was no fault of England's that the eminent culture, political influence, and unapproached legal status of Mr. Reeves should have coincided exactly with her political requirements at that crisis, nor yet that she should have utilized a coincidence which had the double advantage of securing the permanent services, whilst realizing at the same time the life's aspiration, of a distinguished British subject. But that Mr. Froude should be dinning in our ears this case of benefited self-interest, gaining the amplest reciprocity, both as to service and serviceableness, with the disinterested spontaneity of America's elevation of Mr. Douglass, is but another proof of the obliquity of the moral medium through which he is wont to survey mankind and their concerns.

The distinction between the two marvellous careers which we have been discussing demands, as it is susceptible of, still sharper accentuation. In the final success of Reeves, it is the man himself who confronts one in the unique transcendency and victoriousness of personal merit. On the other hand, a million times the personal merit of Reeves combined with his own could have availed Douglass absolutely nothing in the United States, legal and social proscript that he was, with public opinion generally on the side of the laws and usages against him. The very little countries of the world are proverbial for the production of very great men. But, on the other hand, narrowness of space favours the concentration and coherence of the adverse forces that might impede, if they fail of utterly thwarting, the success which may happen to be grudged by those possessing the will and the power for its obstruction. In Barbados, so far as we have heard, read, and seen ourselves of the social ins and outs of that little sister-colony, the operation of the above mentioned

influences has been, may still be, to a certain extent, distinctly appreciable. Although
in English jurisprudence there is no law
ordaining the proscription, on the ground
of race or colour, of any eligible candidate
for social or political advancement, yet is it
notorious that the ethics and practices of the
" Anglo-West Indians " — who, our author
has dared to say, represent the higher type
of Englishmen—have, throughout successive
generations, effectually and of course detri-
mentally operated, as though by a positive
Medo-Persian edict, in a proscriptive sense. It
therefore demanded extraordinary toughness
of constitutional fibre, moral, mental, and, let
us add, physical too, to overcome the obstacles
opposed to the progress of merit, too often
by persons in intelligence below contempt,
but, in prosperity and accepted pretension,
formidable indeed to fight against and overcome. We shudder to think of the petty
cabals, the underbred indignities, direct and
indirect, which the present eminent Judge
had to watch against, to brush aside, to smile
at, in course of his epic strides towards the
highest local pinnacle of his profession. But

with him, as Time has shown, it was all sure and safe.

Providence had endowed him with the powers and temperament that break down, when opportunity offers, every barrier to the progress of the gifted and strong and brave. That opportunity, in his particular case, offered itself in the Confederation crisis. Distracted and helpless " Anglo-West Indians " thronged to him in imploring crowds, praying that their beloved Charter should be saved by the exertion of his incomparable abilities. Save and except Dr. Carrington, there was not a single member of the dominant section in Barbados whom it would not be absurd to name even as a near second to him whom all hailed as the Champion of their Liberties. In the contest to be waged the victory was not, as it never once has been, reserved to the SKIN or pedigree of the combatants. The above two matters, which in the eyes of the ruling "Bims" had, throughout long decades of undisturbed security, been placed before and above all possible considerations, gravitated down to their inherent insignificance when Intellect and Worth were destined to fight out the issue. Mr.

Reeves, whose possession of the essential qualifications was admittedly greater than that of every colleague, stood, therefore, in unquestioned supremacy, lord of the political situation, with the result above stated.

To what we have already pointed out regarding the absolute impossibility of such an opportunity ever presenting itself in America to Mr. Douglass, in a political sense, we may now add that, whereas, in Barbados, for the intellectual equipment needed at the crisis, Mr. Reeves stood quite alone, there could, in the bosom of the Union, even in respect of the gifts in which Mr. Douglass was most brilliant, be no "walking over the course" by him. It was in the country and time of Bancroft, Irving, Whittier, Longfellow, Holmes, Bryant, Motley, Henry Clay, Dan Webster, and others of the laureled phalanx which has added so great and imperishable a lustre to the literature of the English tongue.

We proceed here another step, and take up a fresh deliverance of our author's in reference to the granting of the franchise to the black population of these Colonies. "It is," says Mr. James Anthony Froude, who is just as pro-

phetic as his prototypes, the slave-owners of
the last half-century, "it is as certain as anything future can be, that *if we give the negroes
as a body* the political privileges which *we claim
for ourselves*, they they will use them only to
their own injury." The forepart of the above
citation reads very much as if its author wrote
it on the principle of raising a ghost for the
mere purpose of laying it. What visionary,
what dreamer of impossible dreams, has ever
asked for the Negroes *as a body* the same
political privileges which are claimed for themselves by Mr. Froude and others of his
countrymen, who are presumably capable of
exercising them? No one in the West Indies
has ever done so silly a thing as to ask for
the Negroes as a body that which has not, as
everybody knows, and never will be, conceded
to the people of Great Britain as a body. The
demand for Reform in the Crown Colonies—a
demand which our author deliberately mis-
represents—is made neither by nor for the
Negro, Mulatto, White, Chinese, nor East
Indian. It is a petition put forward by prominent responsible colonists — the majority of
whom are Whites, and mostly Britons besides.

Their prayer, in which the whole population
in these Colonies most heartily join, is simply
and most reasonably that we, the said Colonies,
being an integral portion of the British Empire,
and having, in intelligence and every form of
civilized progress, outgrown the stage of political tutelage, should be accorded some measure
of emancipation therefrom.   And thereby we—
White, Black, Mulatto, and all other inhabitants
and tax-payers—shall be able to protect ourselves against the self-seeking and bold indifference to our interests which seem to be
the most cherished expression of our rulers'
official existence.   It may be possible (for he
has attempted it), that our new instructor in
Colonial ethics and politics, under the impulsion
of skin-superiority, and also of confidence in the
probable success of experiments successfully
tried fifty years before, does really believe in
the sensibleness of separating COLOURS, and
representing the wearers of them as being
generally antagonistic to one another in Her
Majesty's West Indian Dominions.   How is it
then, we may be permitted to ask Mr. Froude,
that no complaint of the sort formulated by
him as against the Blacks has ever been put

forward by the thousands of Englishmen, Scotchmen, Irishmen, and other Europeans who are permanent inhabitants, proprietors, and tax-payers of these Colonies? The reason is that Anglo-West Indianism, or rather Colonialism, is the creed of a few residents sharply divisible into two classes in the West Indies. Labouring conjointly under race-madness, the first believes that, as being of the Anglo-Saxon race, they have a right to crow and dominate in whatever land they chance to find themselves, though in their own country they or their forefathers had had to be very dumb dogs indeed. The Colonial Office has for a long time been responsible for the presence in superior posts of highly salaried gentry of this category, who have delighted in showing themselves off as the unquestionable masters of those who supply them with the pay that gives them the livelihood and position they so ungratefully requite. These fortunate folk, Mr. Froude avers, are likely to leave our shores in a huff, bearing off with them the civilizing influences which their presence so surely guarantees. Go tell to the marines that the seed of Israel flourishing in the borders of

Misraim will abandon their flourishing district
of Goshen through sensitiveness on account of
the idolatry of the devotees of Isis and Osiris!

The second and less placable class of
" Englishmen in the West Indies," whose final
departure our author would have us to believe
would complete the catastrophe to progress in
the British Antilles, is very impalpable indeed.
We cannot feel them.    We have failed to
even see them.    True, Mr. Froude scouts on
their behalf the bare notion of their condescending to meet, on anything like equality,
us, whom he and they pretend (rather ana-
chronistically, at least) to have been their
former slaves, or servants.    But where, in the
name of Heaven, where are these *sortis de la
cuisse de Jupiter*, Mr. Froude ?    If they are
invisible, mourning in impenetrable seclusion
over the impossibility of having, as their fathers
had before them, the luxury of living at the
Negroes' expense, shall we Negroes who are in
the sunshine of heaven, prepared to work and
win our way, be anywise troubled in our Jubilee
by the drivelling ineptitude which insanely re-
minds us of the miseries of those who went
before us ?    We have thus arrived at the car

dinal, essential misrepresentation, out of scores
which compose "The Bow of Ulysses," and
upon which its phrases mainly hinge. *Semper
eadem*—"Always the same" — has been the
proud motto of the mightiest hierarchy that has
controlled human action and shaped the destinies
of mankind, no less in material than in ghostly
concerns. Yet is a vast and very beneficial
change, due to the imperious spirit of the times,
manifest in the Roman Church. No longer do
the stake, the sword, and the dismal horrors of
the interdict figure as instruments for assuring
conformity and submission to her dogmas.
She is now content to rest her claims on her
beneficence in the past, as attested by noble
and imperishable memorials of her solicitude
for the poor and the ignorant, and in proclaim-
ing the gospel without those ghastly coercives
to its acceptance. Surely such a change, however unpalatable to those who have been compelled to make it, is most welcome to the
outside world at large. "Always the same" is
also, or should be, the device of the discredited
herd whose spokesman Mr. Froude is so proud
to be. In nothing has their historical character,
as shown in the published literature of their

cause up to 1838, exhibited any sign of amelio-
ration.   It cannot be affected by the spirit and
the lessons of the times.   Mendacity and a sort
of judicial blindness seem to be the two most
salient characteristics by which are to be distinguished these implacable foes and would-
be robbers of human rights and liberty.   But,
gracious heavens! what can tempt mortals to
incur this weight of infamy?  Wealth and
Power?   To be (very improbably) a Crœsus
or (still more improbably) a Bonaparte, and to
perish at the conventional age, and of vulgar
disease, like both ?   Turpitudes on the part of
sane men, involving the sacrifice of the priceless attributes of humanity, can be rendered
intelligible by the supreme temporal gains
above indicated, but only if exemption from the
common lot of mankind—in the shape of care,
disease, and death—were accompaniments of
those prizes.

In favour of slavery, which has for so many
centuries desolated the African family and
blighted its every chance of indigenous progress—of slavery whose abolition our author
so ostentatiously regrets — only one solitary
permanent result, extending in every case over

a natural human life, has been paraded by him as a respectable justification. At page 246, speaking of Negroes met by him during a stroll which he took at Mandeville, Jamaica, he tells us :—

" The people had black faces ; but even they had shaped their manners in the old English models. The men touched their hats respectfully (as they eminently did not in Kingston and its environs). The women smiled and curtsied, and the children looked shy when one spoke to them. The name of slavery is a horror to us ; but there must have been *something human and kindly* about it, too, when it left upon the character *the marks of courtesy and good breeding*" !

Alas for Africa and the sufferings of her desolated millions, in view of so light-hearted an assessment as this ! Only think of the ages of outrage, misery, and slaughter—of the countless hecatombs that Mammon is hereby absolved from having directly exacted, since the sufficing expiatory outcome of it all has been only "marks of courtesy and good breeding" ! Marks that are displayed, forsooth, by the survivors of the ghastly experiences or by

their descendants! And yet, granting the appreciable ethical value of the hat-touching, the
smirking and curtseyings of those Blacks to
persons whom they had no reason to suspect
of unfriendliness, or whose white face they
may in the white man's country have greeted
with a civility perhaps only prudential, we fail
to discover the necessity of the dreadful agency
we have adverted to, for securing the results
on manners which are so warmly commended.
African explorers, from Mungo Park to Livingstone and Stanley, have all borne sufficient
testimony to the world regarding the natural
friendliness of the Negro in his ancestral home,
when not under the influence of suspicion,
anger, or dread.

It behoves us to repeat (for our detractor is a
persistent repeater) that the cardinal dodge by
which Mr. Froude and his few adherents expect
to succeed in obtaining the reversal of the progress of the coloured population is by misrepre-
senting the elements, and their real attitude
towards one another, of the sections composing
the British West Indian communities. Everybody knows full well that Englishmen, Scotchmen, and Irishmen (who are not officials), as

well as Germans, Spaniards, Italians, Portuguese, and other nationalities, work in unbroken
harmony and, more or less, prosper in these
Islands. These are no cherishers of any vain
hankering after a state of things in which men
felt not the infamy of living not only on the
unpaid labour, but at the expense of the sufferings, the blood, and even the life of their fellow-
men. These men, honourable by instinct
and of independent spirit, depend on their own
resources for self-advancement in the world—
on their capital either of money in their pockets
or of serviceable brains in their heads, energy
in their limbs, and on these alone, either singly
or more or less in combination. These reputable specimens of manhood have created homes
dear to them in these favoured climes ; and
they, at any rate, being on the very best terms
with all sections of the community in which
their lot is cast, have a common cause as
fellow - sufferers under the *régime* of Mr.
Froude's official " birds of passage." The
agitation in Trinidad tells its own tale. There
is not a single black man—though there should
have been many—among the leaders of the
movement for Reform. Nevertheless the honour-

able and truthful author of " The English in the West Indies," in order to invent a plausible pretext for his sinister labours of love on behalf of the poor pro-slavery survivals, and despite his knowledge that sturdy Britons are at the head of the agitation, coolly tells the world that it is a struggle to secure " negro domination."

The further allegation of our author respecting the black man is curious and, of course, dismally prophetic. As the reader may perhaps recollect, it is to the effect that granting political power to the Negroes as a body, equal in scope " to that claimed by Us " (*i.e.*, Mr. Froude and his friends), would certainly result in the use of these powers by the Negroes to their own injury. And wherefore ? If Mr. Froude professes to believe—what is a fact—that there is " no original or congenital difference of capacity" between the white and the African races, where is the consistency of his urging a contention which implies inferiority in natural shrewdness, as regards their own affairs, on the part of black men ? Does this blower of the two extremes of temperature in the same breath pretend that the average British voter is better informed, can see more clearly what is for his own advan-

tage, is better able to assess the relative merits
of persons to be entrusted with the spending
of his taxes, and the general management of
his interests? If Mr. Froude means all this,
he is at issue not only with his own specific
declaration to the contrary, but with facts of
overwhelming weight and number showing pre-
cisely the reverse. We have personally had
frequent opportunities of coming into contact,
both in and out of England, with natives of
Great Britain, not of the agricultural order
alone, but very often of the artisan class, whose
ignorance of the commonest matters was as
dense as it was discreditable to the land of their
birth and breeding. Are these people included
(on account of having his favourite *sine quâ non*
of a fair skin) in the US of this apostle of
skin-worship, in the indefeasible right to political power which is denied to Blacks by reason,
or rather non-reason, of their complexion?

The fact is, that, judging by his own sentiments and those of his Anglo-West Indian
friends, Mr. Froude calculated on producing an
impression in favour of their discreditable views
by purposely keeping out of sight the numerous
European and other sufferers under the yoke

which he sneers at seeing described by its
proper appellation of "a degrading tyranny."
The prescriptive unfavourable forecast of our
author respecting political power in the hands
of the Blacks may, in our opinion, be hailed as
a warrant for its bestowal by those in whose
power that bestowal may be. As a pro-slavery
prophecy, equally dismal and equally confident
with the hundreds that preceded it, this new
vaticination may safely be left to be practically
dealt with by the Race, victimized and maligned,
whose real genius and character are purposely
belied by those who expect to be gainers by
the process. Invested with political power, the
Negroes, Mr. Froude goes on to assure his
readers, "will slide back into their old condition, and the chance will be gone of lifting
them to the level to which we have no right to
say they are incapable of rising." How touch-
ingly sympathetic! How transcendently liberal
and righteous! But, to speak the truth, is not
this solicitude of our cynical defamer on our
behalf, after all, a useless waste of emotion on
his part ? *Timeo Danaos et dona ferentes.*
The tears of the crocodile are most copious in
close view of the banquet on his prey. This

reiterated twaddle of Mr. Froude, in futile and
unseasonable echo of the congenial predictions
of his predecessors in the same line, might be
left to receive not only the answer of his own
book to the selfsame talk of the slavers fifty
years ago, but also that of the accumulated
refutations which America has furnished for
the last twenty-five years as to the retrograde
tendency so falsely imputed.   But, taking it as
a serious contention, we find that it involves a
suggestion that the according of electoral votes
to citizens of a certain complexion would, *per
se* and *ipso facto*, produce a revulsion and
collapse of the entire prevailing organization
and order of a civilized community.

What talismanic virtue this prophet of evil
attributes to a vote in the hand of a Negro out
of Barbados, where for years the black man's
vote has been operating, harmlessly enough,
Heaven knows, we cannot imagine.  At all
events, as sliding back on the part of a community is a matter which would require some
appreciable time, however brief, let us hope
that the authorities charged " to see that the
state receive no detriment" would be vigilant
enough and in time to arrest the evil and vindi-

cate the efficiency of the civilized methods of self-preservation.

Our author concludes by another reference to Chief Justice Reeves: " Let British authority die away, and the average black nature, such as it now is, be left free to assert itself, there will be no more negroes like him in Barbadoes *or anywhere.*" How the dying away of British authority in a British Colony is to come to pass, Mr. Froude does not condescend here explicitly to state. But we are left free to infer from the whole drift of " The English in the West Indies " that it will come through the exodus *en masse* said to be threatened by his " Anglo-West Indians." Mr. Froude sympathetically justifies the disgust and exasperation of these reputable folk at the presence and progress of the race for whose freedom and ultimate elevation Britain was so lavish of the wealth of her noblest intellects, besides paying the prodigious money-ransom of TWENTY MILLION pounds sterling. With regard to our author's talk about " the average black nature, such as it now exists, being left free to assert itself," and the dire consequences therefrom to result, we can only feel pity at the desperate straits to which, in his search for a pretext for gratuitous slander, a man of our author's capacity has been so ignominiously reduced. All we can say to him with reference to this portion of his violent suppositions is that " the average black nature, such as it now exists," should NOT, in a civilized community, be left free to assert itself, any more than the average white, the average brown, the average red, or indeed any average colour of human nature whatsoever. As self-defence is the first law of nature, it has followed that every condition of organized society, however simple or primitive, is furnished with some recognized means of self-protection against the free assertion of itself by the average nature of any of its members.

Of course, if things should ever turn out according to Mr. Froude's desperate hypothesis, it may also happen that there will be no more Negroes like Mr. Justice Reeves in Barbados. But the addition of the words " or anywhere" to the above statement is just another of those suppressions of the truth which, absolutely futile though they are, constitute the only means by which the policy he writes to promote can possibly be made to

appear even tolerable.  The assertion of our
author, therefore, standing as it actually does,
embracing the whole world, is nothing less
than an audacious absurdity, for there stand
the United States, the French and Spanish
Islands—not to speak of the Central and South
American Republics, Mexico, and Brazil—all
thronged with black, mixed blood, and even
half-breed high officials, staring him and the
whole world in the face.

The above noted suppression of the truth to
the detriment of the obnoxious population re-
calls a passage wherein the suggestion of what
is not the truth has been resorted to for the
same purpose.  At page 123 we read: "The
disproportion of the two races—always dangerously large—has increased with ever-gathering
velocity since the emancipation. *It is now
beyond control on the old lines.*"  The use of
the expletive "dangerously," as suggestive of
the truculence of the people to whom it refers,
is critically allowable in view of the main intention of the author.  But what shall we say of the
suggestion contained in the very next sentence,
which we have italicized?  We are required
by it to understand that in slavery-time the

planters had some organized method, rendered impracticable by the Emancipation, of checking, for their own personal safety, the growth of the coloured population. If we, in deference to the superior mental capacity of our author, admit that self-interest was no irresistible motive for promoting the growth of the human " property " on which their prosperity depended, we are yet at liberty to ask what was the nature of the " old lines " followed for controlling the increase under discussion. Was it suffocation of the babes by means of sulphur fumes, the use of beetle-paste, or exposure on the banks of the Caribbean rivers ? In the later case History evidently lost a chance of self-repetition in the person of some leader like Moses, the Hebra-Egyptian Spartacus, arising to avenge and deliver his people.

We now shall note how he proceeds to descant on slavery itself :—" Slavery," says he, " was a survival from a social order which had passed away, and slavery could not be continued. IT DOES NOT FOLLOW THAT *per se* IT WAS A CRIME. The negroes who were sold to the dealers in the factories were most of them either slaves already to worse masters or were *servi*, servants in the old meaning of the word, or else criminals, *servati* or reserved from death. They would otherwise have been killed, and since the slave trade has been abolished, are again killed in the too celebrated customs. . . ."

Slavery, as Mr. Froude and the rest of us are bound to discuss it at present, is by no means susceptible of the gloss which he has endeavoured, in the above extract, to put on it. The British nation, in 1834, had to confront and deal with the only species of slavery which was then within the cognizance of public morals and practical politics. Doubtless our author, learned and erudite as he is, would like to transport us to those patriarchal ages when, under theocratic decrees, the chosen people were authorized to purchase (not to kidnap) slaves, and keep them as an everlasting inheritance in their posterity. The slaves so purchased, we know, became members of the families to which their lot was attached, and were hedged in from cruel usage by distinct and salutary regulations. This is the only species of slavery which—with the addition of the old Germanic self-enslavements and the generally prevailing ancient custom of pledging one's personal services in liquidation of indebtedness—can be covered by the singular verdict of non-criminality which our author has pronounced. He, of course, knows much better than we do what the condition of slaves was in Greece as well as in Rome. He knows, too, that the " wild and guilty phantasy that man could hold property in man," lost nothing of its guilt or its wildness with the lapse of time and the changes of circumstances which overtook and affected those reciprocal relations. Every possibility of deterioration, every circumstance wherein man's fallen nature could revel in its worst inspirations, reached culmination at the period when the interference of the world, decreed by Providence, was rendered imperative by the sufferings of the bondsmen. It is this crisis of the history of human enslavement that Mr. Froude must talk about, if he wishes to talk to any purpose on the subject at all. His scoffs at British ". virtuous benevolence," and his imputation of ingratitude to the Negro in respect of that self-same benevolence, do not refer to any theocratic, self-contracted, abstract, or idyllic condition of servitude. They pin his meaning down to that particular phase when slavery had become not only "the sum," but the very quintessence, "of all human villainies."

At its then phase, slavery had culminated into being a menace, portentous and far-encroaching, to not only the moral life but the very civilization of the higher types of the human family, so debasing and blighting were its effects on those who came into even tolerating contact with its details. The indescribable atrocities practised on the slaves, the deplorable sapping of even respectable principles in owners of both sexes—all these stood forth in their ineffable hideousness before the uncorrupted gaze of the moral heroes, sons of Britain and America, and also of other countries, who, buckling on the armour of civilization and right, fought for the vindication of them both, through every stern vicissitude, and won the first grand, ever-memorable victory of 1838, whereof we so recently celebrated the welcome Jubilee! Oh! it was a combat of archangels against the legions that Mammon had banded together and incited to the conflict. But though it was Sharp, Clarkson, Wilberforce, and the rest of that illustrious host of cultured, lofty-souled, just, merciful, and beneficent men, who were thus the saviours, as well as the servants, of society, yet have we seen it possible for an Englishman of to-day to mouth against their memory the ineptitudes of their long-vanquished foes, and to flout the consecrated dead in their graves, as the Bœotian did the living Pericles in the market-place of Athens !

Why waste words and time on this defamer of his own countrymen, who, on account of the material gain and the questionable martial glory of the conquest, eulogizes Warren Hastings, the viceregal plunderer of India, whilst, in the same breath, he denounces Edmund Burke for upholding the immutable principles of right and justice ! These principles once, and indubitably now, so precious in their fullest integrity to the normal British conscience, must henceforth, say Mr. Froude and his fellow-colonialists, be scored off the moral code of Britain, since they " do not pay " in tangible pelf, in self-aggrandisement, or in dazzling prestige.

The statement that many negroes who were sold to the dealers in the factories were "slaves

already to worse masters" is, in the face of
facts which could not possibly have been un-
known to him, a piece of very daring assertion.
But this should excite no wonder, considering
that precise and scrupulous accuracy would
be fatal to the discreditable cause to which he
so shamelessly proclaims his adhesion.   As
being familiar since early childhood with members of almost every tribe of Africans (mainly
from or arriving by way of the West Coast)
who were brought to our West Indies, we are
in a position to contradict the above assertion
of Mr. Froude's, its unfaltering confidence notwithstanding.   We have had the Madingoes,
Foulahs, Houssas, Calvers, Gallahs, Karamen-
ties, Yorubas, Aradas, Cangas, Kroos, Timnehs,
Vcis, Eboes, Mokoes, Bibis, and Congoes, as
the most numerous and important of the tribal
contribution of Africa to the population of these
Colonies.   Now, from what we have intimately
learned of these people (excepting the Congoes,
who always appeared to us an inferior tribe
to all the others), we unhesitatingly deny that
even three in ten of the whole number were
ever slaves in their own country, in the sense
of having been born under any organized

system of servitude. The authentic records relating to the enslavement of Africans, as a regular systematized traffic, do not date further back than five centuries ago. It is true that a great portion of ancient literature and many monuments bear distinct evidence, all the more impressive because frequently only casual, that, from the earliest ages, the Africans had shared, in common with other less civilized peoples, the doom of having to furnish the menial and servile contingents of the more favoured sections of the human family. Now, dating from, say, five hundred years ago, which was long indeed after the disappearance of the old leading empires of the world, we have (save and except in the case of Arab incursionists into the Eastern and Northern coasts) no reliable authority for saying, or even for supposing, that the tribes of the African interior suffered from the molestations of professional man-hunters.

It was the organization of the West Coast slave traffic towards the close of the sixteenth century, and the extermination of the Caribbean aborigines by Spain, soon after Columbus had discovered the Western Continent, which

gave cohesion, system, impetus, and aggressive-
ness to the trade in African flesh and blood.
Then the factory dealers did not wait at their
seaboard mart, as our author would have us
suppose, for the human merchandize to be
brought down to them.   The *auri sacra fames,*
the accursed craving for gain, was too imperious for that.   From the Atlantic border to
as far inland as their emissaries could penetrate,
their bribes, in every species of exchangeable
commodities, were scattered among the ra-
pacious chiefs on the river banks ; while these
latter, incited as well by native ferocity as by
lust of gain, rushed forth to "make war" on
their neighbours, and to kidnap, for sale to the
white purchaser, every man, woman, and child
they could capture amidst the nocturnal flames,
confusion, tumult, and terror resulting from
their unexpected irruption.   That the poor
people thus captured and sold into foreign
bondage were under *worse masters* than those
under whom they, on being actually bought
and becoming slaves, were doomed to experience all the atrocities that have thrilled
with horror the conscience of the civilized
Christian world, is a statement of worse than

childish absurdity. Every one, except Mr. Froude and his fellow-apologists for slavery, knows that the cruelty of savage potentates is summary, uncalculating, and, therefore, merciful in its ebullitions. A head whisked off, brains dashed out, or some other short form of savage dispatch, is the preferential method of destruction. With our author's better masters, there was the long, dreary vicissitude, beginning from the horrors of the capture, and ending perhaps years upon years after, in some bush or under the lash of the driver. The intermediate stages of the starvation life of hunger, chains, and hideous exposure at the barancoon, the stowing away like herrings on board the noisome ship, the suffocation, the deck-sores wrought into the body by the attrition of the bonier parts of the system against the unyielding wood—all these, says Mr. Froude, were more tolerable than the swift doing away with life under an African master! Under such, at all events, the care and comfort suitable to age were strictly provided for, and cheered the advanced years of the faithful bondsman.

After a good deal of talk, having the same logical value, our author, in his enthusiasm for

slavery, delivers himself thus: " For myself,
I would rather be the slave of a Shakespeare
or a Burghley, than the slave of a majority in the
House of Commons, or the slave of my own
folly." Of the four above specified alternatives
of enslavement, it is to be regretted that temperament, or what is more likely, perhaps, self-
interest, has driven him to accept the fourth,
or the latter of the two deprecated yokes, his
book being an irrefutable testimony to the fact.
For, most assuredly, it has not been at the
prompting of wisdom that a learned man of
unquestionably brilliant talents and some
measure of accorded fame could have prosti-
tuted those talents and tarnished that fame
by condescending to be the literary spokesman
of the set for whose miserable benefit he
recommends the statesmen of his country to
perjure and compromise themselves, regardless
of inevitable consequences, which the value of
the sectional satisfaction to be thereby given
would but very poorly compensate. Possibly
a House of Commons majority, whom this
dermatophilist evidently rates far lower than
his " Anglo-West Indians," might, if he were
their slave, have protected their own self-

respect by restraining him from vicariously scandalizing them by his effusions.

After this curious boast about his preferences as a hypothetic bondsman, Mr. Froude proceeds gravely to inform his readers that "there may be authority yet not slavery; a soldier is not a slave, a wife is not a slave . . ." and he continues, with a view of utilizing these platitudes against the obnoxious Negro, by telling us that persons sustaining the above specified and similar relations "may not live by their own wills, or emancipate themselves at their own pleasure from positions in which nature has placed them, or into which they have themselves voluntarily entered. The negroes of the West Indies are children, and not yet disobedient children. . . . If you enforce self-government upon them when they are not asking for it, you may . . . wilfully drive them back into the condition of their ancestors, *from which the slave-trade was the beginning of their emancipation*"! The words which we have signalized by italics in the above extract could have been conceived only by a bigot—such an atrocious sentiment being possible only as the product of mind or morals

wrenched hopelessly out of normal action. All
the remainder of this hashing up of pointless
commonplaces has for its double object a
*suggestio falsi* against us Negroes as a body,
and a diverting of attention, as we have proved
before, from the numerous British claimants of
Reform, whose personality Mr. Froude and his
friends would keep out of view, provided their
crafty policy has the result of effectually re-
pressing the hitherto irrepressible, and, as such,
to the " Anglo-West Indian," truly detestable
Negro.

# West Indian Confederation.

In heedless formulation of his reasons, if such they should be termed, for urging tooth and nail the non-according of reform to the Crown-governed Colonies, our author puts forth this dogmatic deliverance (p. 123) :—

"A West Indian self-governing dominion is possible only with a full Negro vote. If the whites are to combine, so will the blacks. It will be a rule by the blacks and for the blacks."

That a constitution for any of our diversely populated Colonies which may be fit for it is possible only with "a full Negro vote" (to the extent within the competence of such voting), goes without saying, as must be the case with every section of the Queen's subjects eligible for the franchise. The duly qualified Spaniard,

Coolie, Portuguese, or man of any other non-
British race, will each thus have a vote, the
same as every Englishman or any other Briton.
Why, then, should the vote of the Negro be
so especially a bugbear? It is because the
Negro is the game which our political sports-
man is in full chase of, and determined to hunt
down at any cost. Granted, however, for the
sake of argument, that black voters should pre-
ponderate at any election, what then? We are
gravely told by this latter-day Balaam that " If
the whites are to combine, so will the blacks,"
but he does not say for what purpose.

His sentence, therefore, may be legitimately
constructed in full for him in the only sense
which is applicable to the mutual relations
actually existing between those two directly
specified sections of British subjects who he
would fain have the world believe live in a
state of active hostility :—" If the whites are
to combine *for the promotion of the general
welfare, as many of the foremost of them have
done before and are doing now, so will the
blacks also combine in the support of such whites,
and as staunch auxiliaries equally interested
in the furtherance of the same ameliorative*

*objects."* Except in the sense embodied in the
foregoing sentence, we cannot, in these days,
conceive with what intent persons of one
section should so specially combine as to
compel combination on the part of persons of
any other. The further statement that a confederation having a full black voting-power
would be a government " *by* the blacks and *for*
the blacks," is the logical converse of the now
obsolete doctrine of Mr. Froude's inspirers—
" a government by whites should be only for
whites." But this formula, however strenuously
insisted on by those who gave it shape, could
never, since even before three decades from
the first introduction of African slaves, be
thoroughly put in practice, so completely had
circumstances beyond man's devising or control
compelled the altering of men's minds and
methods with regard to the new interests
which had irresistibly forced themselves into
importance as vital items in political arrangements. Nowadays, therefore, that Mr. Froude
should desire to create a state of feeling which
had, and could have had, no existence with
regard to the common interests of the inhabitants for upwards of two full centuries, is

12

evidently an excess of confidence which can only be truly described as amazing. But, after all, what does our author mean by the words "a government by the blacks"? Are we to understand him as suggesting that voting by black electors would be synonymous with electing black representatives? If so, he has clearly to learn much more than he has shown that he lacks, in order to understand and appreciate the vital influences at work in West Indian affairs. Undoubtedly, being the spokesman of the few who (secretly) avow themselves to be particularly hostile to Ethiopians, he has done no more than reproduce their sentiments. For, conscious, as these hankerers after the old "institutions" are, of being utterly ineligible for the furthering of modern progressive ideas, they revenge themselves for their supersession on everybody and everything, save and except their own arrogant stolidity. White individuals who have part and lot in the various Colonies, with their hearts and feelings swayed by affections natural to their birth and earliest associations; and Whites who have come to think the land of their adoption as dear to themselves as the land of their birth, entertain no such dread of

their fellow-citizens of any other section, whom
they estimate according to intelligence and
probity, and not according to any accident of
exterior physique.  Every intelligent black is
as shrewd regarding his own interests as our
author himself would be regarding his in the
following hypothetical case : Some fine day,
being a youth and a bachelor, he gets wedded,
sets up an establishment, and becomes the
owner of a clipper yacht.  For his own service
in the above circumstances we give him the
credit to believe that, on the persons specified
below applying among others to him for employment, as chamber-maid and house-servant,
and also as hands for the vessel, he would, in
preference to any ordinarily recommended white
applicants, at once engage the two black servant-
girls at President Churchill's in Dominica, the
droghermen there as able seamen, and as cabin-
boy the lad amongst them whose precocious
marine skill he has so warmly and justly ex-
tolled.  It is not because all these persons are
black, but because of the soul-consciousness of
the selector, that they each (were they even
blue) had a title to preferential consideration,
his experience and sense of fitness being

their most effectual supporters. Similarly, the Negro voter would elect representatives whom he knew he could trust for competency in the management of his affairs, and not persons whose sole recommendation to him would be the possession of the same kind of skin. Nor, from what we know of matters in the West Indies, do we believe that any white man of the class we have eulogized would hesitate to give his warmest suffrage to any black candidate who he knew would be a fitting representative of his interests. We could give examples from almost every West Indian island of white and coloured men who would be indiscriminately chosen as their candidate by either section. But the enumeration is needless, as the fact of the existence of such men is too notorious to require proof.

Mr. Froude states plainly enough (p. 123) that, whereas a whole thousand years were needed to train and discipline the Anglo-Saxon race, yet " European government, European instruction, continued steadily till his natural tendencies are superseded by a higher instinct, may shorten the probation period of the negro." Let it be supposed that this period of probation for the Negro should extend, under such exceptionally favourable circumstances, to any period less than that which is alleged to have been needed by the Anglo-Saxon to attain his political manhood—what then are the prospects held out by Mr. Froude to us and our posterity on our mastering the training and discipline which he specially recommends for Blacks? Our author, in view, doubtless, of the rapidity of our onward progress, and indeed our actual advancement in every respect, thus answers (pp. 123–4) :—" Let a generation or two pass by *and carry away with them the old traditions*, and an English governor-general will be found presiding over a black council, delivering the speeches made for him by a black prime minister ; and how long could this endure ?   No English gentleman would consent to occupy so absurd a situation."

And again, more emphatically, on the same point (p. 285) :—" No Englishman, not even a bankrupt peer, would consent to occupy such a position ; the blacks themselves would despise him if he did ; and if the governor is to be one of their own race and colour, how long would such a connection endure ? "

It is plainly to be seen from the above two extracts that the political ethics of our author, being based on race and colour exclusively, would admit of no conceivable chance of real elevation to any descendant of Africa, who, being Ethiopian, could not possibly change his skin. The "old traditions" which Mr. Froude supposes to be carried away by his hypothetical (white) generations who have "passed by," we readily infer from his language, rendered impossible such incarnations of political absurdity as those he depicts. But what should be thought of the sense, if not indeed the sanity, of a grave political teacher who prescribes "European government" and "European education" as the specifics to qualify the Negro for political emancipation, and who, when these qualifications are conspicuously mastered by the Negro who has undergone the training, refuses him the prize, *because* he is a Negro? We see further that, in spite of being fit for election to council, and even to be prime ministers competent to indite governors' messages, the pigment under our epidermis dooms us to eventual disappointment and a life-long condition of contempt. Even so is it

desired by Mr. Froude and his clients, and not
without a spice of piquancy is their opinion
that for a white ruler to preside and rule over
and accept the best assistance of coloured men,
qualified as above stated, would be a self-
degradation too unspeakable for toleration by
any Englishman—"even a bankrupt peer."
Unfortunately for Mr. Froude, we can point him
to page 56 of this his very book, where, speaking of Grenada and deprecating the notion of
its official abandonment, our author says :—

"Otherwise they [Negroes] were quiet fellows,
and if the politicians would only let them alone,
they would be perfectly contented, and might
eventually, if wisely managed, come to some
good. . . . *Black* the island was, and *black* it
would remain. *The conditions were never likely
to arise which would bring back a European
population;* but a governor *who was a sensible
man*, who would reside and use his natural
influence, could manage it with perfect ease."

Here, then, we see that the governor of an
entirely black population may be a sensible
man, and yet hold the post. Our author, indeed, gives the Blacks over whom this sensible
governor would hold rule as being in number

just 40,000 souls ; and we are therefore bound
to accept the implied suggestion that the dis-
honour of holding supremacy over persons of
the odious colour begins just as their number
begins to count onward from 40,000 !   There
is quite enough in the above verbal vagaries of
our philosopher to provoke a volume of comment.   But we must pass on to further clauses of
this precious paragraph.   Mr. Froude's talent
for eating his own words never had a more
striking illustration than here, in his denial of
the utility of native experience as the safest
guide a governor could have in the administration of Colonial affairs.   At page 91 he says :—
" Among the public servants of Great Britain
there are persons always to be found fit and
willing for *posts of honour and difficulty*, if a
sincere effort be made to find them."

A post of honour and difficulty, we and all
other persons in the British dominions had all
along understood was regarded as such in the
case of functionaries called upon to contend
with adverse forces in the accomplishment
of great ends conceived by their superiors.
But we find that, according to Mr. Froude, all
the credit that has hitherto redounded to those

who had succeeded in such tasks has been
in reality nothing more than a gilding over
of disgrace, whenever the exertions of such
officials had been put forth amongst persons
not wearing a European epidermis. The extension of British influence and dominion over
regions inhabited by races not white is therefore, on the part of those who promote it, a
perverse opening of arenas for the humiliation
and disgrace of British gentlemen, nay, even of
those titled members of the " black sheep "
family—bankrupt peers! As we have seen,
however, ample contradiction and refutation
have been considerately furnished by the same
objector in this same volume, as in his praises
of the governor just quoted.

The cavil of Mr. Froude about English
gentlemen reading messages penned by black
prime ministers applies with double force to
English barristers (who are *gentlemen* by statute)
receiving the law from the lips of black judges.
For all that, however, an emergency arose
so pressing as to compel even the colonialism
of Barbados to practically and completely refute
this doctrine, by praying for, and submitting
with gratitude to, the supreme headship of a

man of the race which our author so finically depreciates.   In addition it may be observed that for a governor to even consult his prime minister in the matter of preparing his mes-sages might conceivably be optional, whilst it is obligatory on all barristers, whether English or otherwise, to defer to the judge's interpretation of the law in every case—appeal afterwards being the only remedy.   As to the dictum that "the two races are not equal and will not blend," it is open to the fatal objection that, having himself proved, with sympathizing pathos, how the West Indies are now well-nigh denuded of their Anglo-Saxon inhabitants, Mr. Froude would have us also understand that the miserable remnant who still complainingly in-habit those islands must, by doing violence to the understanding, be taken as the whole of the world-pervading Anglo-Saxon family.   The Negroes of the West Indies number a good deal more than two million souls.   Does this suggester of extravagances mean that the prejudices and vain conceit of the few dozens whom he champions should be made to over-ride and overbear, in political arrangements, the serious and solid interests of so many hundreds of thousands ? That " the two races are not equal " is a statement which no sane man would dispute, but acquiescence in its truth involves also a distinct understanding that the word race, as applied in the present case by our author, is a simple accommodation of terms —a fashion of speech having a very restricted meaning in this serious discussion.

The Anglo-Saxon race pervades Great Britain, its cradle, and the Greater Britain extending almost all over the face of the earth, which is the arena of its activities and marvellous achievements. To tell us, therefore, as Mr. Froude does, that the handful of malcontents whose unrespectable grievance he holds up to public sympathy represents the Anglo-Saxon race, is a grotesque *façon de parler*. Taking our author's "Anglo-West Indians" and the people of Ethiopian descent respectively, it would not be too much to assert, nor in anywise difficult to prove by facts and figures, that for every competent individual of the former section in active civilized employments, the coloured section can put forward at least twenty thoroughly competent rivals. Yet are these latter the people whom the classic Mr.

Froude wishes to be immolated, root and branch, in all their highest and dearest interests, in order to secure the maintenance of "old traditions" which, he tells us, guaranteed for the dominant cuticle the sacrifice of the happiness of down-trodden thousands ! Referring to his hypothetical confederation with its black office-holders, our author scornfully asks :—

"And how long would this endure ? "

The answer must be that, granting the existence of such a state of things, its duration would be not more nor less than under white functionaries. For according to himself (p. 124): " There is no original or congenital difference of capacity between " the white and black races, and "with the same chances and the same treatment, . . . distinguished men would be produced equally from both races."

If, therefore, the black ministers whose hue he so much despises do possess the training and influence rendering them eligible and securing their election to the situations we are considering, it must follow that their tenure of office would be of equal duration with that of individuals of the white race under the same conditions. Not content with making himself the mouthpiece of English gentlemen in this matter, our author, with characteristic hardihood, obtrudes himself into the same post on behalf of Negroes ; saying that, in the event of even a bankrupt peer accepting the situation of governor-general over them, "The blacks themselves would despise him"!

Mr. Froude may pertinently be asked here the source whence he derived his certainty on this point, inasmuch as it is absolutely at variance with all that is sensible and natural ; for surely it is both foolish and monstrous to suppose that educated men would infer the degradation of any one from the fact of such a one consenting to govern and co-operate with themselves for their own welfare. He further asks on the same subject :—

"And if the governor is to be one of their own race and colour, how long could such a connection endure ?"

Our answer must be the same as with regard to the duration of the black council and black prime minister carrying out the government under the same conditions. It must be regretted that no indication in his book, so far as it professes to deal with facts and with persons not within the circle of his clients, would justify a belief that its wanton misstatements have filtrated through a mind entitled to declare, with the authority of self-consciousness, what a gentleman would or would not do under given circumstances.

In reiteration of his favourite doctrine of the antagonism between the black and white races, our author continues on the same page to say :—

"No one, I presume, would advise that the whites of the island should govern. *The relations between the two populations are too embittered*, and equality once established by law, *the exclusive privilege of colour over colour* cannot be restored. *While slavery continued, the whites ruled effectively and economically;* the blacks are now as they."

As far as could possibly be endeavoured, every proof has been crowded into this book in refutation of this favourite allegation of Mr. Froude's. It is only an idle waste of time to be thus harping on his colour topic. No one can deserve to govern simply because he is white, and no one is bound to be subject simply because he is black. The whole of West

Indian history, even after the advent of the attorney-class, proves this, in spite of the efforts to secure exclusive white domination at a time when crude political power might have secured it.

" The relations between the two populations are too embittered," says Mr. Froude. No doubt his talk on this point would be true, had any such skin-dominancy as he contemplates been officially established ; but as at present most officials are appointed (locally at least) according to their merit, and not to their epidermis, nothing is known of the embittered relations so constantly dinned into our ears. Whatever bitterness exists is in the minds of those gentry who would like to be dominant on the cheap condition of showing a simple bodily accident erected by themselves into an evidence and proof of superiority.

" The exclusive privilege of colour over colour cannot be restored." Never in the history of the British West Indies—must we again state—was there any law or usage establishing superiority in privileges for any section of the community on account of colour. This statement of fact is also and again an answer to, and refutation of, the succeeding allegation that, "While slavery continued, the *whites ruled* effectively and economically." It will be yet more clearly shown in a later part of this essay that during slavery, in fact for upwards of two centuries after its introduction, the West Indies were ruled by *slave-owners*, who happened to be of all colours, the means of purchasing slaves and having a plantation being the one exclusive consideration in the case. It is, therefore, contrary to fact to represent the Whites exclusively as ruling, and the Blacks indiscriminately as subject.

He goes on to say, "There are two classes in the community; their interests are opposite as they are now understood." As regards the above, Mr. Froude's attention may be called to the fact that classification in no department of science has ever been based on colour, but on relative affinity in certain salient qualities. To use his own figure, no horse or dog is more or less a horse or dog because it happens to be white or black. No teacher marshals his pupils into classes according to any outward physical distinction, but according to intellectual approximation. In like manner there has been wealth for hundreds of men of Ethiopic origin, and poverty for hundreds of men of Caucasian origin, and the reverse in both cases. We have, therefore, had hundreds of black as well as white men who, under providential dispensation, belonged to the class, rich men ; while, on the other hand, we have had hundreds of white men who, under providential dispensation, belonged to the class, poor men. Similarly, in the composition of a free mixed community, we have hundreds of both races belonging to the class, competent and eligible ; and hundreds of both races belonging to the class, incompetent and ineligible : to both of which classes all possible colours might belong. It is from the first mentioned that are selected those who are to bear the rule, to which the latter class is, in the very nature of things, bound to be subject. There is no government by reason merely of skins. The diversity of individual intelligence and circumstances is large enough to embrace the possibility of even children being, in emergencies, the most competent influencers of opinion and action.

But let us analyse this matter for just a while more. The fatal objection to all Mr. Froude's advocacy of colour-domination is that

it is futile from being morally unreasonable.
In view of the natural and absolute impossibility of reviving the same external conditions
under which the inordinate deference and submission to white persons were both logically
and inevitably engendered and maintained, his
efforts to talk people into a frame of mind
favourable to his views on this subject are but
a melancholy waste of well-turned sentences.
Man's estimate of his fellow-man has not and
never can have any other standard, save and
except what is the outcome of actual circumstances influencing his sentiment. In the
primitive ages, when the fruits of the earth
formed the absorbing object of attention and
interest, the men most distinguished for successful culture of the soil enjoyed, as a consequence,
a larger share than others of popular admiration
and esteem. Similarly, among nomadic tribes,
the hunters whose courage coped victoriously
with the wild and ferocious denizens of the
forest became the idols of those who witnessed
and were preserved by such sylvan exploits.
When men came at length to venture in ships
over the trackless deep in pursuit of commerce
and its gains, the mariner grew important in

public estimation. The pursuit of commerce and its gains led naturally to the possession of wealth. This, from the quasi-omnipotence with which it invests men — enabling them not only to command the best energies, but also, in many cases, to subvert the very principles of their fellows—has, in the vast majority of cases, an overpowering sway on human opinion : a sway that will endure till the Millennium shall have secured for the righteous alone the sovereignty of the world. Likewise, as cities were founded and constitutions established, those who were foremost as defenders of the national interests, on the field of bodily conflict or in the intellectual arena, became in the eyes of their contemporaries worthiest of appreciation—and so on of other circumstances through which particular personal distinctions created claims to preference.

In the special case of the Negroes kidnapped out of Africa into foreign bondage, the crowning item in their assessment of their alien enslavers was the utter superiority, over their most re-doubtable " big men," which those enslavers dis-played. They actually subjugated and put in chains, like the commonest peasants, native

potentates at whose very names even the warrior-
hood of their tribes had been wont to blench.
But far surpassing even this in awful effect was
the doom meted out to the bush-handlers, the
medicine-men, the rain-compellers, erewhile so
inscrutably potent for working out the bliss
or the bale of friend or enemy. " Lo, from no
mountain-top, from no ceiba-hollow in the forest
recesses, has issued any interposing sign, any
avenging portent, to vindicate the Spirit of
Darkness so foully outraged in the hitherto
inviolate person of his chosen minister! Verily,
even the powers of the midnight are impotent
against these invaders from beyond the mighty
salt-water!  Here, huddled together in confused, hopeless misery and ruin, lie, fettered
and prostrate, even priest as well as potentate, undistinguishable victims of crude, un-
blenching violence, with its climax of nefarious
sacrilege.  We, common mortals, therefore, can
hope for no deliverance from, or even succour
in, the woful plight thus dismally contrived for
us all by the fair-skinned race who have now
become our masters." Such was naturally the
train of thought that ran through those forlorn
bosoms.  The formidable death-dealing guns

of the invaders, the ships which had brought them to the African shores, and much besides in startling contrast to their own condition of utter helplessness, the Africans at once interpreted to themselves as the manifestation and inherent attributes of beings of a higher order than man. Their skin, too, the difference whereof from their own had been accentuated by many calamitous incidents, was hit upon as the reason of so crushing an ascendency.

White skin therefore became, in those disconsolate eyes, the symbol of fearful irresistible power: which impression was not at all weakened afterwards by the ineffable atrocities of the "middle-passage." Backed ultimately by their absolute and irresponsible masterhood at home over the deported Blacks, the European abductors could easily render permanent in the minds of their captives the abject terror struck into them by the enormities of which they had been the victims. Now, the impressions we touched upon before bringing forward the case of the Negro slaves were mainly produced by pleasurable circumstances. But of a contrary nature and much more deeply graven are those sentiments which are the outcome of hopeless terror

and pain. For whilst impressions of the former
character glide into the consciousness through
accesses no less normal than agreeable, the in-
fusion of fear by means of bodily suffering is a
process too violent to be forgotten by minds
tortured and strained to unnatural tension thereby. Such tension, oft-recurrent and scarcely
endurable, leaves behind it recollections which
are in themselves a source of sadness. But
time, favoured by a succession of pleasurable
experiences, is a sovereign anodyne to remem-
brances of this poignant class. No wonder,
then, from our foregoing detail of facts, that
whiteness of skin was both redoubted and
tremblingly crouched to by Negroes on whom
Europeans had wrought such unspeakable
calamities. Time, however, and the action of
circumstances, especially in countries subject to
Catholic dominion, soon began to modify the
conditions under which this sentiment of terror
had been maintained, and, with those conditions, the very sentiment itself. For it was
not long in the life of many of the expa-
triated Africans before members of their own
race obtained freedom, and, eventually, wealth
sufficient for purchasing black slaves on their

own account. In other respects, too (outwardly at least), the prosperous career of such individual Blacks could not fail to induce a revulsion of thought, whereby the attribution of unapproachable powers exclusively to the Whites became a matter earnestly reconsidered by the Africans. Centuries of such reconsideration have produced the natural result in the West Indies. With the daily competition in intelligence, refinement, and social and moral distinction, which time and events have brought about between individuals of the two races, nothing, surely, has resulted, nor has even been indicated, to re-infuse the ancient colour-dread into minds which had formerly been forced to entertain it ; and still less to engender it in bosoms to which such a feeling cannot, in the very nature of things, be an inborn emotion. Now, can Mr. Froude show us by what process he would be able to infuse in the soul of an entire population a sentiment which is both unnatural and beyond compulsion ?

The foregoing remarks roughly apply to pre-eminence given to outward distinction, and the conditions under which mainly it impresses and is accepted by men not yet arrived at the essentially intellectual stage. In the spiritual domain the conditions have ever been quite different. A belief in the supernatural being inborn in man, the professors of knowledge and powers beyond natural attainment were by common consent accorded a distinct and superior consideration, deemed proper to the sacredness of their progression. Hence the supremacy of the priestly caste in every age and country of the world. Potentate as well as peasant have bowed in reverence before it, as representing and declaring with authority the counsels of that Being whom all, priest, potentate and peasant alike, acknowledge and adore, each according to the measure of his inward illumination.

# The Negro as a Worker.

———◦◦◦———

The laziness, the incurable idleness, of the Negro, was, both immediately before their emancipation in 1838, and for long years after that event, the cuckoo-cry of their white detractors. It was laziness, pure and simple, which hindered the Negro from exhausting himself under a tropical sun, toiling at starvation wages to ensure for his quondam master the means of being an idler himself, with the additional luxury of rolling in easily come-by wealth. Within the last twenty years, however, the history of the Black Man, both in the West Indies and, better still, in the United States of America, has been a succession of achievements which have converted the charge of laziness into a baseless and absurd calumny. The repetition of the charge referred to is, in these

waning days of the nineteenth century, a discredited anachronism, which, however, has no
deterring features for Mr. Froude. As the
running down of the Negro was his cue, he
went in boldly for the game, with what result
we shall presently see. At page 239, our
author, speaking of the Negro garden-farms in
Jamaica, says :—

" The male proprietors were *lounging about*
smoking. Their wives, as it was market-day,
were tramping into Kingston with their baskets
on their heads. We met them literally in
thousands, all merry and light-hearted, their
little ones with little baskets trudging at their
side. Of the *lords of the creation* we saw,
perhaps, one to each hundred of the women,
and he would be riding on mule or donkey, pipe
in mouth and *carrying nothing*. He would be
generally *sulky* too, while the ladies, young and
old, had a civil word for us, and curtsied under
their loads. Decidedly if there is to be a black
constitution I will give my vote to the women."

To the above direct imputation of indolence,
heartlessness, and moroseness, Mr. Froude
appends the following remarks on other moral
characteristics of certain sable peasants at

Mandeville, Jamaica, given on the authority of a police official, who, our author says, described them as—

"Good-humoured, but not universally honest. They stole cattle, and would not give evidence against each other. If brought into Court, they held a pebble in their mouth, being under the impression that when they were so provided, perjury did not count. *Their education was only skin-deep, and the schools which the Government provided had not touched their characters at all.*"

But how could the education so provided be otherwise than futile when the administration of its details is entirely in the hands of persons unsympathizing with and utterly despising the Negro? But of this more anon and elsewhere. We resume Mr. Froude's evidence respecting the black peasantry. Our author proceeds to admit, on the same subject, that his informant's duties (as a police official) "brought him in contact with the unfavourable specimens." He adds :—

"I received a far pleasanter impression from a Moravian minister. . . . I was particularly glad to see this gentleman, for of the Moravians

every one had spoken well to me.   He was not
the least enthusiastic about his poor black sheep,
but he said that if they were not better than the
average English labourer, he did not think them
worse.    They were called idle ; *they would work
well enough if they had fair wages and if the
wages were paid regularly ; but what could be
expected when women servants had but three
shillings a week and found themselves, when the
men had but a shilling a day and the pay was
kept in arrear in order that if they came late to
work, or if they came irregularly, it may be kept
back or cut down to what the employer choose to
give ?   Under such conditions* ANY *man of* ANY
*colour would prefer to work for himself if he
had a garden, or would be idle if he had none."*

Take, again, the following extract regarding
the heroism of the emigrants to the Canal :—

" I walked forward " (on the steamer bound
to Jamaica), " after we had done talking.   We
had five hundred of the poor creatures on their
way to the Darien pandemonium.   The vessel
was rolling with a heavy beam sea.   I found the
whole mass of them reduced to the condition
of the pigs who used to occupy the fore decks
on the Cork and Bristol packets.   They were

lying in a confused heap together, helpless,
miserable, without consciousness, apparently,
save a sense in each that he was wretched.
Unfortunate brothers-in-law ! following the laws
of political economy, and carrying their labour
to the dearest market, where, before a year was
out, half of them were to die. They *had souls*,
too, *some of* them, and honest and kindly hearts."

It surely is refreshing to read the revelation
of his first learning of the possession of a soul
by a fellow-human being, thus artlessly described
by one who is said to be an ex-parson. But
piquancy is Mr. Froude's strong point, whatever
else he may be found wanting in.

Still, apart from Mr. Froude's direct testimony to the fact that from year to year, during
a long series of years, there has been a continuous, scarcely ever interrupted emigration
of Negroes to the Spanish mainland, in search
of work for a sufficing livelihood for themselves and their families—and that in the
teeth of physical danger, pestilence, and death—
there would be enough indirect exoneration of
the Black Man from that indictment in the wail
of Mr. Froude and his friends regarding the
alarming absorption of the lands of Grenada

and Trinidad by sable proprietors. Land cannot be bought without money, nor can money
be possessed except through labour, and the
fact that so many tens of thousand Blacks are
now the happy owners of the soil whereon, in
the days so bitterly regretted by our author,
their forefathers' tears, nay, very hearts' blood,
had been caused to flow, ought to silence for
ever an accusation, which, were it even true,
would be futile, and, being false, is worse than
disgraceful, coming from the lips of the Eu-
molpids who would fain impose a not-to-be-
questioned yoke on us poor helots of Ethiopia.
It is said that lying is the vice of slaves ; but
the ethics of West Indian would-be mastership
assert, on its behalf, that they alone should
enjoy the privilege of resorting to misrepresentation to give colour, if not solidity, to their
pretensions.

# Religion for Negroes.

Mr. Froude's passing on from matters secular
to matters spiritual and sacred was a transition
to be expected in the course of the grave and
complicated discussion which he had volunteered
to initiate. It was, therefore, not without
curiosity that his views in the direction above
indicated were sought for and earnestly scru-
tinized by us. But worse than in his treatment
of purely mundane subjects, his attitude here
is marked by a nonchalant levity which excites
our wonder that even he should have touched
upon the spiritual side of his thesis at all. The
idea of the dove sent forth from the ark fluttering
over the heaving swells of the deluge, in vain
endeavour to secure a rest for the soles of its
feet, represents not inaptly the unfortunate pre-
dicament of his spirit with regard to a solid

faith on which to repose amid the surges of
doubt by which it is so evidently beset. Yet
although this is his obvious plight with regard
to a satisfying belief, he nevertheless undertakes, with characteristic confidence, to suggest
a creed for the moralization of West Indian
Negroes. His language is :—

" A religion, at any rate, which will keep the
West Indian blacks from falling back into
devil-worship is still to seek. In spite of the
priests, child-murder and cannibalism have re-
appeared in Hayti, but without them things
might have been much worse than they are, and
the preservation of white authority and influence
in any form at all may be better than none."

We discern in the foregoing citation the
exercise of a charity that is unquestionably
born of fetish-worship, which, whether it be
obeah generally, or restricted to a mere human
skin, can be so powerful an agent in the forma-
tion and retention of beliefs. Hence we see
that our philosopher relies here, in the domain
of morals and spiritual ethics, on a white skin
as implicitly as he does on its sovereign potency
in secular politics. The curiousness of the
matter lies mainly in its application to natives

of Hayti, of all people in the world. As a matter of fact we have had our author declaring as follows, in climax to his oft-repeated predictions about West Indian Negroes degenerating into the condition of their fellow-Negroes in the " Black Republic " (p. 285) :—

"Were it worth while, one might draw a picture of an English governor, with a black parliament and a black ministry, recommending, by advice of his constitutional ministers, some measure like the Haytian Land Law."

Now, as the West Indies degenerating into so many white-folk-detesting Haytis, under our prophet's dreaded supremacy of the Blacks, is the burden of his book ; and as the Land Law in question distinctly forbids the owning by any white person of even one inch of the soil of the Republic, it might, but for the above explanation, have seemed unaccountable, in view of the implacable distrust, not to say hatred, which this stern prohibition so clearly discloses, that our author should, nevertheless, rely on the efficacy of *white* authority and influence over Haytians.

In continuation of his religious suggestions, he goes on to descant upon slavery in the

14

fashion which we have elsewhere noticed, but
it may still be proper to add a word or two here
regarding this particular disquisition of his.
This we are happy in being able to do under
the guidance of an anterior and more reliable
exponent of ecclesiastical as well as secular
obedience on the part of all free and enlightened men in the present epoch of the
world's history :—

> " Dogma and Descent, potential twin
> Which erst could rein submissive millions in,
> Are now spent forces on the eddying surge
> Of Thought enfranchised.   Agencies emerge
> Unhampered by the incubus of dread
> Which cramped men's hearts and clogged their
>         onward tread.
> Dynasty, Prescription ! spectral in these days
> When Science points to Thought its surest ways,
> And men who scorn obedience when not free
> Demand the logic of Authority !
> The day of manhood to the world is here,
> And ancient homage waxes faint and drear.
>
> .      .      .      .      .      .
>
> Vision of rapture !   See Salvation's plan
> —'Tis serving God through ceaseless toil for man ! "

The lines above quoted are by a West
Indian Negro, and explain in very concise
form the attitude of the educated African mind

with reference to the matters they deal with.
Mr. Froude is free to perceive that no special
religion patched up from obsolete creeds could
be acceptable to those with whose sentiments
the thoughts of the writer just quoted are in
true racial unison. It is preposterous to expect that the same superstition regarding skin
ascendency, which is now so markedly played
out in our Colonies in temporal matters, could
have any weight whatsoever in matters so
momentous as morals and religion. But granting even the possibility of any code of worldly
ethics or of religion being acceptable on the
dermal score so strenuously insisted on by
him, it is to be feared that, through sheer
respect for the fitness of things, the intelligent
Negro in search of guidance in faith and morals
would fail to recognize in our author a guide,
philosopher, and friend, to be followed without
the most painful misgivings. The Catholic
and the Dissenting Churches which have done
so much for the temporal and spiritual advancement of the Negro, in spite of hindrance and
active persecution wherever these were possible,
are, so far as is visible, maintaining their hold
on the adhesion of those who belong to them.

And it cannot be pretended that, among enlightened Africans as compared with other
enlightened people, there have been more
grievous fallings off from the scriptural standard of deportment.   Possible it certainly is
that considerations akin to, or even identical
with, those relied upon by Mr. Froude might,
on the first reception of Christianity in their
exile, have operated effectually upon the minds
of the children of Africa.   At that time the
evangelizers whose converts they so readily
became possessed the recommendation of belonging to the dominant caste.   Therefore, with
the humility proper to their forlorn condition,
the poor bondsmen requited with intense gratitude such beneficent interest on their behalf,
as a condescension to which people in their
hapless situation could have had no right.   But
for many long years, the distinction whether of
temporal or of spiritual superiority has ceased
to be the monopoly of any particular class.   The
master and employer has for far more than a
century and a half been often represented in
the West Indies by some born African or his
descendant ; and so also has the teacher and
preacher.   It is not too much to say that

the behaviour of the liberated slaves throughout the British Antilles, as well as the deportment of the manumitted four million
slaves of the Southern United States later on,
bore glorious testimony to the humanizing
effects which the religion of charity, clutched
at and grasped in fragments, and understood
with childlike incompleteness, had produced
within those suffering bosoms.

Nothing has occurred to call for a remodelling
of the ordinary moral and spiritual machinery
for the special behoof of Negroes. Religion,
as understood by the best of men, is purely
a matter of feeling and action between man
and man—the doing unto others as we would
they should do unto us ; and any creed or any
doctrine which directly or indirectly subverts
or even weakens this basis is in itself a danger
to the highest welfare of mankind. The simple
conventional faith in God, in Jesus, and in a
future state, however modified nowadays, has
still a vitality which can restrain and ennoble
its votaries, provided it be inculcated and received in a befitting spirit. Our critic, in the
plenitude of his familiarity with such matters,
confidently asks :—

"Who is now made wretched by the fear of hell ?"

Possibly the belief in the material hell, the decadence of which he here triumphantly assumes to be so general, may have considerably diminished; but experience has shown that, with the advance of refinement, there is a concurrent growth in the intensity of moral sensibility, whereby the waning terrors of a future material hell are more than replaced by the agonies of a conscience self-convicted of wilful violation of the right. The same simple faith has, in its practical results, been rich in the records of the humble whom it has exalted ; of the poor to whom it has been better than wealth ; of the rich whose stewardship of worldly prosperity it has sanctified ; of the timid whom it has rendered bold ; and of the valiant whom it has raised to a divine heroism —in fine, of miracles of transformation that have impelled to higher and nobler tendencies and uses the powers and gifts inherited or acquired by man in his natural state. They who possess this faith, and cherish it as a priceless possession, may calmly oppose to the philosophic reasoning against the existence of

a Deity and the rationalness of entreating Him
in prayer, the simple and sufficient declaration,
" I believe." Normal-minded men, sensible of
the limitations of human faculties, never aspire
to be wise beyond what is revealed. Whatever
might exist beyond the grave is, so far as man
and man in their mutual relations are concerned,
not a subject that discussion can affect or speculation unravel. To believers it cannot matter
whether the Sermon on the Mount embodies or
does not embody the quality of ethics that the
esoteric votaries of Mr. Froude's " new creed "
do accept or even can tolerate. Under the old
creed man's sense of duty kindled in sympathy
towards his brother, urging him to achieve
by self-sacrifice every possibility of beneficence ; hence the old creed insured an inward
joy as well as "the peace which passeth all
understanding." There can be no room for
desiring left, when receptiveness of blessings
overflows ; and it is the worthiest direction of
human energy to secure for others that fulness
of fruition. Is not Duty the first, the highest
item of moral consciousness ; and is not promoting, according to our best ability, the
welfare of our fellow-creatures, the first and

most urgent call of human duty? Can the urgency of such responsibility ever cease but with the capacity, on our own or on our brother's part, to do or be done by respectively? Contemptuously ignoring his share of this solemn responsibility—solemn, whether regarded from a religious or a purely secular point of view—to observe at least the negative obligation never to wantonly do or even devise any harm to his fellows, or indeed any sentient creature, our new apostle affords, in his light-hearted reversal of the prescriptive methods of civilized ethics, a woful foretaste of the moral results of the " new, not as yet crystallized " belief, whose trusted instruments of spiritual investigation are the telescope and mental analysis, in order to satisfy the carpings of those who so impress the world with their super-human strong-mindedness.

The following is a profound reflection presenting, doubtless, quite a new revelation to an unsophisticated world, which had so long submitted in reverential tameness to the self-evident impossibility of exploring the Infinite :—

" The tendency of popular thought is against

the supernatural in any shape. Far into space
as the telescope can search, deep as analysis can
penetrate into mind and consciousness or the
forces which govern natural things, popular
thought finds only uniformity and connection of
cause and effect; no sign anywhere of a personal will which is influenced by prayer or
moral motives."

How much to be pitied are the gifted
esoterics who, in such a quest, vainly point
their telescopes into the star-thronged firma-
ment, and plunge their reasoning powers into
the abyss of consciousness and such-like
mysteries! The commonplace intellect of the
author of "Night Thoughts" was, if we may
so speak, awed into an adoring rapture which
forced from him the exclamation (may believers
hail it as a dogma!) —

"An undevout astronomer is mad!"

Most probably it was in weak submission to
some such sentiment as this that Isaac Newton
nowhere in his writings suggests even the ghost
of a doubt of there being a Great Architect
of the Universe as the outcome of his tele-
scopic explorations into the illimitable heavens.

It is quite possible, too, that he was, "on in-
sufficient grounds," perhaps, perfectly satisfied,
as a host of other intellectual mediocrities like
himself have been, and even up to now rather
provokingly continue to be, with the very
"uniformity and connection of cause and
effect" as visible evidence of there being not
only "a personal will," but a creative and
controlling Power as well.   In this connection
comes to mind a certain old Book which, whatever damage Semitic Scholarship and Modern
Criticism may succeed in inflicting on its
contents, will always retain for the spiritual
guidance of the world enough and to spare
of divine suggestions.   With the prescience
which has been the heritage of the inspired
in all ages, one of the writers in that Book,
whom we shall now quote, foresaw, no doubt,
the deplorable industry of Mr. Froude and his
*protégé* "popular thought," whose mouth-piece
he has so characteristically constituted himself,
and asks in a tone wherein solemn warning
blends with inquiry : "Canst thou by searching
find out God ; canst thou find out the Almighty
unto perfection !"   The rational among the
most loftily endowed of mankind have grasped

the sublime significance of this query, acquiescing reverently in its scarcely veiled in-
timation of man's impotence in presence of the
task to which it refers.

But though Mr. Froude's spiritual plight be
such as we have just allowed him to state it,
with regard to an object of faith and a motive
of worship, yet let us hear him, in his anxiety
to furbish up a special Negro creed, setting
forth the motive for being in a hurry to antici-
pate the "crystallization" of his new belief:—

"The new creed, however, not having
crystallized as yet into a shape which can
be openly professed, and as without any creed
at all the flesh and the devil might become too
powerful, we maintain the old names, as we
maintain the monarchy."

The allusion to the monarchy seems not a
very obvious one, as it parallels the definitive
rejection of a spiritual creed with the theo-
retical change of ancient notions regarding
a concrete fact. At any rate we have it that
his special religion, when concocted and dis-
seminated, will have the effect of preventing
the flesh and the devil from having too much
power over Negroes. The objection to the

devil's sway seems to us to come with queer grace from one who owes his celebrity chiefly to the production of works teeming with that peculiar usage of language of which the Enemy of Souls is credited with the special father-hood.

No, sir, in the name of the Being regarding whose existence you and your alleged "popular thought" are so painfully in doubt, we protest against your right, or that of any other created worm, to formulate for the special behoof of Negroes any sort of artificial creed unbelieved in by yourself, having the function and effect of detective "shadowings" of their souls. Away with your criminal suggestion of toleration of the hideous orgies of heathenism in Hayti for the benefit of our future morals in the West Indies, when the political supremacy which you predict and dread and deprecate shall have become an accomplished fact. Were any special standard of spiritual excellence required, our race has, in Josiah Henson and Sojourner Truth, sufficing models for our men and our women respectively. Their ideal of Christian life, which we take to be the true one, is not to be judged of with direct reference to the Deity whom we cannot

see, interrogate, or comprehend, but to its practical bearing in and on man, whom we can see
and have cognizance of, not only with our
physical senses, but by the intimations of the
divinity which abides within us.[1]  We can see,
feel, and appreciate the virtue of a fellow-mortal
who consecrates himself to the Divine idea
through untiring exertion for the bettering
of the condition of the world around him,
whose agony he makes it his duty, only to
satisfy his burning desire, to mitigate.  The
fact in its ghastly reality lies before us that the
majority of mankind labour and are being
crushed under the tremendous trinity of Ignorance, Vice, and Poverty.

  It is mainly in the succouring of those who
thus suffer that the vitality of the old creed
is manifested in the person of its professors.
Under this aspect we behold it moulding men,
of all nations, countries, and tongues, whose
virtues have challenged and should command
on its behalf the unquestioning faith and
adhesion of every rational observer. "Evidences of Christianity," "Controversies,"
"Exegetical Commentaries," have all proved

  [1] "Est deus in nobis, agitante calescimus illo."—*Ovid.*

more or less futile—as perhaps they ought—
with the Science and Modern Criticism which
perverts religion into a matter of dialectics.
But there is a hope for mankind in the fact that
Science itself shall have ultimately to admit the
limitations of human inquiry into the details of
the Infinite. Meanwhile it requires no technical
proficiency to recognize the criminality of those
who waste their brief threescore and ten years
in abstract speculations, while the tangible,
visible, and hideous soul-destroying trinity of
Vice, Ignorance, and Poverty, above mentioned, are desolating the world in their very
sight. There are possessors of personal virtue,
enlightenment, and wealth, who dare stand
neutral with regard to these dire exigencies
among their fellows. And yet they are the
logical helpers, as holders of the special antidote
to each of those banes! Infinitely more deserving of execration are such folk than the
callous owner of some specific, who allows a
suffering neighbour to perish for want of it.

We who believe in the ultimate development of the Christian notion of duty towards
God, as manifested in untiring beneficence to
man, cling to this faith—starting from the

beginning of the New Testament dispensation—because Saul of Tarsus, transformed into
Paul the Apostle through his whole-souled
acceptance of this very creed with its practical responsibilities, has, in his ardent, inde-
fatigable labours for the enlightenment and
elevation of his fellows, left us a lesson which
is an enduring inspiration ; because Augustine,
Bishop of Hippo, benefited, in a manner which
has borne, and ever will bear, priceless fruit,
enormous sections of the human family, after
his definite submission to the benign yoke
of the same old creed ; because Vincent de
Paul has, through the identical inspiration,
endowed the world with his everlasting legacy
of organized beneficence ; because it impelled
Francis Xavier with yearning heart and eager
footsteps through thousands of miles of peril,
to proclaim to the darkling millions of India
what he had experienced to be tidings of
great joy to himself ; because Matthew Hale, a
lawyer, and of first prominence in a pursuit
which materializes the mind and nips its
native candour and tenderness, escaped un-
blighted, through the saving influence of his
faith, approving himself in the sight of all

an ideal judge, even according to the highest
conception ; because John Howard, opulent
and free to enjoy his opulence and repose, was
drawn thereby throughout the whole continent
of Europe in quest of the hidden miseries
that torture those whom the law has shut out,
in dungeons, from the light and sympathy of the
world ; because Thomas Clarkson, animated by
the spirit of its teachings, consecrated wealth,
luxury, and the quiet of an entire lifetime on
the altar of voluntary sacrifice for the salvation
of an alien people ; because Samuel Johnson,
shut out from mirthfulness by disease and suffering, and endowed with an intellectual pride
intolerant of froward ignorance, was, through
the chastening power of that belief, transformed
into the cheerful minister and willing slave of
the weaklings whom he gathered into his home,
and around whom the tendrils of his heart had
entwined themselves, waxing closer and stronger
in the moisture of his never-failing charity ;
because Henry Havelock, a man of the sword,
whose duties have never been too propitious to
the cultivation and fostering of the gentler virtues,
lived and died a blameless hero, constrained by
that faith to be one of its most illustrious ex-

emplars ; because David Livingstone looms great and reverend in our mental sight in his devotion to a land and race embraced in his boundless fellow-feeling, and whose miseries he has commended to the sympathy of the civilized world in words the pathos whereof has melted thousands of once obdurate hearts to crave a share in applying a balm to the " open sore of Africa "—that slave-trade whose numberless horrors beggar description; and finally—one more example out of the countless varieties of types that blend into a unique solidarity in the active manifestation of the Christian life—we believe because Charles Gordon, the martyr-soldier of Khartoum, in trusting faith a very child, but in heroism more notable than any mere man of whom history contains a record, gathered around himself, through the sublime attractiveness of his faith-directed life, the united suffrages of all nations, and now enjoys, as the recompense and seal of his life's labours, an apotheosis in homage to which the heathen of Africa, the man-hunting Arab, the Egyptian, the Turk, all jostle each other to blend with the exulting children of Britain who are directly glorified by his life and history.

Here, then, are speaking evidences of the believers' grounds.   Verily they are of the kind that are to be seen in our midst, touched, heard, listened to, respected, beloved—nay, honoured, too, with the glad worship our inward spirit springs forth to render to goodness so largely plenished from the Source of all Good.   Can Modern Science and Criticism explain them away, or persuade us of their insufficiency as incentives to the hearty acceptance of the religion that has received such glorious, yet simply logical, incarnation in the persons of weak, erring men who welcomed its responsibilities conjointly with its teachings, and thereby raised themselves to the spiritual level pictured to ourselves in our conception of angels who have been given the Divine charge concerning mankind.   Religion for Negroes, indeed! White priests, forsooth!   This sort of arrogance might, possibly, avail in quarters where the person and pretensions of Mr. Froude could be impressive and influential—but here, in the momentous concern of man with Him who "is no respecter of persons," his interference, mentally disposed as he tells us he is with reference to such a matter, is nothing less than profane intrusion.

We will conclude by stating in a few words
our notion of the only agency by which, not
Blacks alone, but every race of mankind, might
be uplifted to the moral level which the thousands of examples, of which we have glanced
at but a few, prove so indubitably the capacity of man to attain — each to a degree
limited by the scope of his individual powers.
The priesthood whereof the world stands in
such dire need is not at all the confederacy
of augurs which Mr. Froude, perhaps in re-
collection of his former profession, so glibly
suggests, with an esoteric creed of their own,
"crystallized into shape" for profession before
the public. The day of priestcraft being now
numbered with the things that were, the ex-
ploitation of those outside of the sacerdotal
circle is no longer possible. Therefore the religion of mere talk, however metaphysical and
profound ; the religion of scenic display, except
such display be symbolic of living and active
verities, has lost whatever of efficacy it may
once have possessed, through the very spirit
and tendency of To-day. The reason why those
few whom we have mentioned, and the thousands who cannot possibly be recalled, have, as

typical Christians, impressed themselves on the moral sense and sympathy of the ages, is simply that they lived the faith which they professed. Whatever words they may have employed to express their serious thoughts were never otherwise than, incidentally, a spoken fragment of their own interior biography. In fine, success must infallibly attend this special priesthood (whether episcopally " ordained " or not) of all races, all colours, all tongues whatsoever, since their lives reflect their teachings and their teachings reflect their lives. Then, truly, they, "the righteous, shall inherit the earth," leading mankind along the highest and noblest paths of temporal existence. Then, of course, the obeah, the cannibalism, the devil-worship of the whole world, including that of Hayti, which Mr. Froude predicts will be adopted by us Blacks in the West Indies, shall no more encumber and scandalize the earth.

But Mr. Froude should, at the same time, be reminded that cannibalism and the hideous concomitants which he mentions are, after all, relatively minor and restricted dangers to man's civilization and moral soundness. They can neither operate freely nor expand easily. The paralysis of horrified popular sentiment obstructs their propagation, and the blight of the death-penalty which hangs over the heads of their votaries is an additional guarantee of their being kept within bounds that minimize their perniciousness. But there are more fatal and further-reaching dangers to public morality and happiness of which the regenerated current opinion of the future will take prompt and remedial cognizance. Foremost among these will be the circulation of malevolent writings whereby the equilibrium of sympathy between good men of different races is sought to be destroyed, through misleading appeals to the weaknesses and prejudices of readers ; writings in which the violation of actual truth cannot, save by stark stupidity, be attributed to innocent error ; writings that scoff at humanitarian feeling and belittle the importance of achievements resulting therefrom ; writings which strike at the root of national manliness, by eulogizing brute force directed against weaker folk as a fit and legitimate mode of securing the wishes of a mighty and enlightened people ; writings, in fine, which ignore the divine prin-

ciple in man, and implicitly deny the possibility
of a Divine Power existing outside of and above
man, thus materializing the mind, and tending
to render the earth a worse hell than it ever
could have been with faith in the supremacy of
a beneficent Power.

BOOK IV.

# Résumé.

———◆———

Thus far we have dealt with the main questions raised by Mr. Froude on the lines of his own choosing; lines which demonstrate to the fullest how unsuited his capacity is for appreciating —still less grappling with—the political and social issues he has so confidently undertaken to determine. In vain have we sought throughout his bastard philosophizing for any phrase giving promise of an adequate treatment of this important subject. We find paraded ostentatiously enough the doctrine that in the adjustment of human affairs the possession of a white skin should be the strongest recommendation. Wonder might fairly be felt that there is no suggestion of a corresponding advantage being accorded to the possession of a long nose or of auburn hair. Indeed, little or no attention that can be deemed serious is given to the interest of the Blacks, as a large and (out of Africa) no longer despicable section of the human family, in the great world-problems which are so visibly preparing and press for definitive solutions.   The intra-African Negro is clearly powerless to struggle successfully against personal enslavement, annexation, or volunteer forcible " protection" of his territory. What, we ask, will in the coming ages be the opinion and attitude of the extra-African millions—ten millions in the Western Hemisphere—dispersed so widely over the surface of the globe, apt apprentices in every conceivable department of civilized culture ?   Will these men remain for ever too poor, too isolated from one another for grand racial combinations ? Or will the naturally opulent cradle of their people, too long a prey to violence and unholy greed, become at length the sacred watchword of a generation willing and able to conquer or perish under its inspiration ?   Such large and interesting questions it was within the province and duty of a famous historian, laying confident claim to prophetic insight, not to propound alone, but also definitely to solve.   The sacred power

of forecast, however, has been confined to
finical pronouncements regarding those for
whose special benefit he has exercised it, and
to childish insults of the Blacks whose doom
must be sealed to secure the precious result
which is aimed at. In view of this ill-inten-
tioned omission, we shall offer a few cursory
remarks bearing on, but not attempting to
answer, those grave inquiries concerning the
African people. As in our humble opinion
these are questions paramount to all the petty
local issues finically dilated on by the confident
prophet of " The Bow of Ulysses," we will here
briefly devote ourselves to its discussion.

Accepting the theory of human development
propounded by our author, let us apply it to the
the African race. Except, of course, to in-
telligences having a share in the Councils of
Eternity, there can be no attainable knowledge
respecting the laws which regulate the growth
and progress of civilization among the races
of the earth. That in the existence of the
human family every age has been marked by
its own essential characteristics with regard
to manifestations of intellectual life, however
circumscribed, is a proposition too self-evident

to require more than the stating. But investigation beyond such evidence as we possess concerning the past—whether recorded by man himself in the written pages of history, or by the Creator on the tablets of nature—would be worse than futile. We see that in the past different races have successively come to the front, as prominent actors on the world's stage. The years of civilized development have dawned in turn on many sections of the human family, and the Anglo-Saxons, who now enjoy pre-eminence, got their turn only after Egypt, Assyria, Babylon, Greece, Rome, and others had successively held the palm of supremacy. And since these mighty empires have all passed away, may we not then, if the past teaches aught, confidently expect that other racial hegemonies will arise in the future to keep up the ceaseless progression of temporal existence towards the existence that is eternal? What is it in the nature of things that will oust the African race from the right to participate, in times to come, in the high destinies that have been assigned in times past to so many races that have not been in anywise superior to us in the qualifications, physical, moral, and intellectual, that mark out a race for prominence amongst other races ?

The normal composition of the typical Negro has the testimony of ages to its essential soundness and nobility. Physically, as an active labourer, he is capable of the most protracted exertion under climatic conditions the most exhausting. By the mere strain of his brawn and sinew he has converted waste tracts of earth into fertile regions of agricultural bountifulness. On the scenes of strife he has in his savage state been known to be indomitable save by the stress of irresistible forces, whether of men or of circumstances. Staunch in his friendship and tender towards the weak directly under his protection, the unvitiated African furnishes in himself the combination of native virtue which in the land of his exile was so prolific of good results for the welfare of the whole slave-class. But distracted at home by the sudden irruptions of skulking foes, he has been robbed, both intellectually and morally, of the immense advantage of Peace, which is the mother of Progress. Transplanted to alien climes, and through centuries of desolating trials, this irrepressible race has bated not one throb of its energy, nor one jot of its heart or hope. In modern times, after his expatriation into dismal bondage, both Britain and America have had occasion to see that even in the paralysing fetters of political and social degradation the right arm of the Ethiop can be a valuable auxiliary on the field of battle. Britain, in her conflict with France for supremacy in the West Indies, did not disdain the aid of the sable arms that struck together with those of Britons for the trophies that furnished the motives for those epic contests.

Later on, the unparalleled struggle between the Northern and Southern States of the American Union put to the test the indestructible fibres of the Negro's nature, moral as well as physical. The Northern States, after months of hesitating repugnance, and when taught at last by dire defeats that colour did not in any way help to victory, at length sullenly acquiesced in the comradeship, hitherto disdained, of the eager African contingent. The records of Port Hudson, Vicksburg, Morris Island, and elsewhere, stand forth in imperishable attestation of the fact that the distinction of being laurelled during life as victor, or filling

in death a hero's grave, is reserved for no
colour, but for the heart that can dare and the
hand that can strike boldly in a righteous cause.
The experience of the Southern slave-holders,
on the other hand, was no less striking and
worthy of admiration.  Every man of the twelve
seceding States forming the Southern Confederacy, then fighting desperately for the avowed
purpose of perpetuating slavery, was called into
the field, as no available male arm could be
spared from the conflict on their side.  Plantation owner, overseer, and every one in authority,
had to be drafted away from the scene of
their usual occupation to the stage whereon the
bloody drama of internecine strife was being
enacted.  Not only the plantation, but the
home and the household, including the mistress
and her children, had to be left, not unprotected,
it is glorious to observe, but, with confident
assurance in their loyalty and good faith, under
the protection of the four million of bondsmen,
who, through the laws and customs of these
very States, had been doomed to lifelong
ignorance and exclusion from all moralizing
influences.  With what result? The protraction
of the conflict on the part of the South would

have been impossible but for the admirable management and realization of their resources by those benighted slaves. On the other hand, not one of the thousands of Northern prisoners escaping from the durance of a Southern captivity ever appealed in vain for the assistance and protection of a Negro. Clearly the head and heart of those bondsmen were each in its proper place. The moral effect of these experiences of the Negroes' sterling qualities was not lost on either North or South. In the North it effaced from thousands of repugnant hearts the adverse feelings which had devised and accomplished so much to the Negro's detriment. In the South—but for the blunders of the Reconstructionists—it would have considerably facilitated the final readjustment of affairs between the erewhile master and slave in their new-born relations of employer and employed.

Reverting to the Africans who were conveyed to places other than the States, it will be seen that circumstances amongst them and in their favour came into play, modifying and lightening their unhappy condition. First, attention must be paid to the patriotic solidarity existing amongst the bondsmen, a solidarity which, in the case of those who had been deported in the same ship, had all the sanctity of blood-relationship. Those who had thus travelled to the "white man's country" addressed and considered each other as brothers and sisters. Hence their descendants for many generations upheld, as if consanguineous, the modes of address and treatment which became hereditary in families whose originals had travelled in the same ship. These adopted uncles, aunts, nephews, nieces, were so united by common sympathies, that good or ill befalling any one of them intensely affected the whole connection. Mutual support commensurate with the area of their location thus became the order among these people. At the time of the first deportation of Africans to the West Indies to replace the aborigines who had been decimated in the mines at Santo Domingo and in the pearl fisheries of the South Caribbean, the circumstances of the Spanish settlers in the Antilles were of singular, even romantic, interest.

The enthusiasm which overflowed from the crusades and the Moorish wars, upon the discovery and conquest of America, had occasioned the peopling of the Western Archipelago by a race of men in whom the daring of freebooters was strangely blended with a fierce sort of religiousness. As holders of slaves, these men recognized, and endeavoured to their best to give effect to, the humane injunctions of Bishop Las Casas. The Negroes, therefore, male and female, were promptly presented for admission by baptism into the Catholic Church, which always had stood open and ready to welcome them. The relations of god-father and god-mother resulting from these baptismal functions had a most important bearing on the reciprocal stations of master and slave. The god-children were, according to ecclesiastical custom, considered in every sense entitled to all the protection and assistance which were within the competence of the god-parents, who, in their turn, received from the former the most absolute submission. It is easy to see that the planters, as well as those intimately connected with them, in assuming such obligations with their concomitant responsibilities, practically entered into bonds which they all regarded as, if possible, more solemn than the natural ties of secular parentage. The duty

of providing for these dependents usually took
the shape of their being apprenticed to, and
trained in the various arts and vocations that
constitute the life of civilization. In many cases,
at the death of their patrons, the bondsmen who
were deemed most worthy were, according to
the means of the testator, provided for in a
manner lifting them above the necessity of
future dependence. Manumission, too, either
by favour or through purchase, was allowed the
fullest operation. Here then was the active
influence of higher motives than mere greed of
gain or the pride of racial power mellowing the
lot and gilding the future prospects of the
dwellers in the tropical house of bondage.

The next, and even more effectual agency
in modifying and harmonizing the relations between owner and bondspeople was the inevitable
attraction of one race to the other by the sentiment of natural affection. Out of this sprang
living ties far more intimate and binding on the
moral sense than even obligations contracted in
deference to the Church. Natural impulses
have often diviner sources than ecclesiastical
mandates. Obedience to the former not seldom
brings down the penalties of the Church; but

the culprit finds solace in the consciousness
that the offence might in itself be a protection
from the thunders it has provoked.　Under
these circumstances the general body of planters,
who were in the main adventurers of the freest
type, were fain to establish connections with such
of the slave-women as attracted their sympathy,
through personal comeliness or aptitude in
domestic affairs, or, usually, both combined.
There was ordinarily in this beginning of the
seventeenth century no Vashti that needed
expulsion from the abode of a plantation Aha-
suerus to make room for the African Esther
to be admitted to the chief place within
the portals.　One great natural consequence
of this was the extension to the relatives or
guardians of the bondswoman so preferred of
an amount of favour which, in the case of the
more capable males, completes the parallel we
have been drawing by securing for each of them
the precedence and responsibilities of a Mor-
decai.　The offspring of these natural alliances
came in therefore to cement more intimately
the union of interests which previous relations
had generated.　Beloved by their fathers, and
in many cases destined by them to a lot superior

to that whereto they were entitled by formal
law and social prescription, these young pro-
creations—Mulattos, as they were called—
were made the objects of special and careful
provisions on the fathers' part. They were,
according to the means of their fathers in the
majority of cases, sent for education and
training to European or other superior institutions. After this course they were either
formally acknowledged by their fathers, or, if
that was impracticable, amply and suitably
provided for in a career out of their native
colony. To a reflecting mind there is something that interests, not to say fascinates, in
studying the action and reaction upon one
another of circumstances in the existence of
the Mulatto. As a matter of fact, he had much
more to complain of under the slave system
than his pure-blooded African relations. The law,
by decreeing that every child of a freeman and a
slave woman must follow the fortune of the womb,
thus making him the property of his mother
exclusively, practically robbed him before his
very birth of the nurture and protection of a
father. His reputed father had no obligation to
be even aware of his procreation, and neverthe-

less—so inscrutable are the ways of Providence !
—the Mulatto was the centre around which
clustered the outraged instincts of nature in
rebellion against the desecrating mandates that
prescribed treason to herself. Law and society
may decree ; but in our normal humanity there
throbs a sentiment which neutralizes every
external impulse contrary to its promptings.

In meditating on the varied history of the
Negro in the United States, since his first
landing on the banks of the James River in
1619 till the Emancipation Act of President
Lincoln in 1865, it is curious to observe that
the elevation of the race, though in a great
measure secured, proceeded from circumstances
almost the reverse of those that operated so
favourably in the same direction elsewhere.
The men of the slave-holding States, chiefly
Puritans or influenced by Puritanic surroundings, were not under the ecclesiastical sway
which rendered possible in the West Indies and
other Catholic countries the establishment of
the reciprocal bonds of god-parents and god-
children. The self-same causes operated to
prevent any large blending of the two races,
inasmuch as the immigrant from Britain who

had gone forth from his country to better his
fortune had not left behind him his attachment
to the institutions of the mother-land, among
which marrying, whenever practicable, was one of
the most cherished.    Above all, too, as another
powerful check at first to such alliances between
the ruling and servile races of the States, there
existed the native idiosyncracy of the Anglo-
Saxon.    That class of them who had left
Britain were likelier than the more refined of
their nation to exhibit in its crudest and cruellest
form the innate jealousy and contempt of other
races that pervades the Anglo-Saxon bosom.    It
is but a simple fact that, whenever he condescended thereto, familiarity with even the love-
liest of the subject people was regarded as a
mighty self-unbending for which the object
should be correspondingly grateful.    So there
could, in the beginning, be no frequent instances
of the romantic chivalry that gilded the quasi-
marital relations of the more fervid and humane
members of the Latin stock.

But this kind of intercourse, which in the
earlier generation was undoubtedly restricted in
North America by the checks above adverted
to, and, presumably, also by the mutual unin-

telligibility in speech, gradually expanded with
the natural increase of the slave population.
The American-born, English-speaking Negro
girl, who had in many cases been the play-
mate of her owner, was naturally more intelligible, more accessible, more attractive—
and the inevitable consequence was the extension apace of that intercourse, the offspring whereof became at length so visibly
numerous.

Among the Romans, the grandest of all
colonizers, the individual's *Civis Romanus sum*
—I am a Roman citizen—was something more
than verbal vapouring; it was a protective
talisman—a buckler no less than a sword.
Yet was the possession of this noble and
singular privilege no barrier to Roman citizens
meeting on a broad humanitarian level any
alien race, either allied to or under the protection of that world-famous commonwealth.
In the speeches of the foremost orators and
statesmen among the conquerors of the then
known world, the allusions to subject or allied
aliens are distinguished by a decorous observ-
ance of the proprieties which should mark any
reference to those who had the dignity of Rome's

friendship, or the privilege of her august protection. Observations, therefore, regarding individuals of rank in these alien countries had the same sobriety and deference which marked allusions to born Romans of analogous degree. Such magnanimity, we grieve to say, is not characteristic of the race which now replaces the Romans in the colonizing leadership of the world. We read with feelings akin to despair of the cheap, not to say derogatory, manner in which, in both Houses of Parliament, native potentates, especially of non-European countries, are frequently spoken of by the hereditary aristocracy and the first gentlemen of the British Empire. The inborn racial contempt thus manifested in quarters where rigid self-control and decorum should form the very essence of normal deportment, was not likely, as we have before hinted, to find any mollifying ingredient in the settlers on the banks of the Mississippi. Therefore should we not be surprised to find, with regard to many an illicit issue of "down South," the arrogance of race so overmastering the promptings of nature as to render not unfrequent at the auction-block the sight of many a chattel of mixed blood, the offspring of some planter whom business exigency had forced to this commercial transaction as the readiest mode of self-release. Yet were the exceptions to this rule enough to contribute appreciably to the weight and influence of the mixed race in the North, where education and a fair standing had been clandestinely secured for their children by parents to whom law and society had made it impossible to do more, and whom conscience rendered incapable of stopping at less.

From this comparative sketch of the history of the slaves in the States, in the West Indies and countries adjacent, it will be perceived that in the latter scenes of bondage everything had conspired to render a fusion of interests between the ruling and the servile classes not only easy, but inevitable. In the very first generation after their introduction, the Africans began to press upward, a movement which every decade has accelerated, in spite of the changes which supervened as each of the Colonies fell under British sway. Nearly two centuries had by this time elapsed, and the coloured influence, which had grown with their wealth, education, numbers, and unity, though circumscribed by the emancipation of the slaves, and the consequent depression in fortune of all slave-owners, never was or could be annihilated. In the Government service there were many for whom the patronage of god-parents or the sheer influence of their family had effected an entrance. The prevalence and potency of the influences we have been dilating upon may be gauged by the fact that personages no less exalted than Governors of various Colonies—of Trinidad in three authentic cases—have been sharers in the prevailing usages, in the matter of standing sponsors (by proxy), and also of relaxing in the society of some fascinating daughter of the sun from the tension and wear of official duty. In the three cases just referred to, the most careful provision was made for the suitable education and starting in life of the issues. For the god-children of Governors there were places in the public service, and so from the highest to the lowest the humanitarian intercourse of the classes was confirmed.

Consequent on the frequent abandonment of their plantations by many owners who despaired of being able to get along by paying their way, an opening was made for the insinuation of Absenteeism into our agricultural, in short, our economic existence. The powerful sugar lords, who had invested largely in the cane plantations, were fain to take over and cultivate the properties which their debtors doggedly refused to continue working, under pretext of the entire absence, or at any rate unreliability, of labour. The representatives of those new transatlantic estate proprietors displaced, but never could replace, the original cultivators, who were mostly gentlemen as well as agriculturists. It was from this overseer class that the vituperations and slanders went forth that soon became stereotyped, concerning the Negro's incorrigible laziness and want of ambition—those gentry adjusting the scale of wages, not according to the importance and value of the labour done, but according to the scornful estimate which they had formed of the Negro personally. And when the wages were fixed fairly, they almost invariably sought to indemnify themselves for their enforced justice by the insulting license of their tongues, addressed to males and females alike. The influence of such men on local legislation, in which they had a preponderating share, either as actual proprietors or as the attorneys of absentees, was not in the direction of refinement or liberality. Indeed, the kind of laws which they enacted, especially during the apprenticeship (1834-8), is thus summarized by one, and him an English officer, who was a visitor in those agitated days of the Colonies :—

" It is demonstrated that the laws which were to come into operation immediately on expiration of the apprenticeship are of the most objectionable character, and fully established the fact not only of a future intention to infringe the rights of the emancipated classes, but of the actual commencement and extensive progress of a Colonial system for that purpose. The object of the laws is to circumscribe the market for free labour––to prohibit the possession or sale of ordinary articles of produce on sale, the obvious intention of which is to confine the emancipated classes to a course of agricultural servitude—to give the employers a monopoly of labour, and to keep down a free competition for wages—to create new and various modes of apprenticeship for the purpose of prolonging predial service, together with many evils of the late system—to introduce unnecessary restraint and coercion, the design of which is to create a perpetual surveillance over the liberated negroes, and to establish a legislative despotism. The several laws passed are based upon the most vicious principles of legislation, and in their operation will be found intolerably oppressive and entirely subversive of the just intentions of the British Legislature."

These liberal-souled gentry were, in sooth, Mr. Froude's "representatives" of Britain, whose traditions steadily followed in their families, he has so well and sympathetically set forth.

We thus see that the irritation and rancour seething in the breast of the new plantocracy, of whom the majority was of the type that then also flourished in Barbados, Jamaica, and Demerara, were nourished and kept acute in order to crush the African element. Harm was done, certainly ; but not to the ruinous extent sometimes declared. It was too late for perfect success, as, according to the Negroes' own phrase, people of colour had by that time already " passed the lock-jaw " [1] stage (at which trifling misadven-

---

[1] " *Yo té'ja passé mal machoè* "—in metaphorical allusion to new-born infants who have lived beyond a certain number of days.

tures might have nipped the germ of their progress in the bud.)   In spite of adverse legislation, and in spite of the scandalous subservience of certain Governors to the Colonial Legislatures, the Race can point with thankfulness and pride to the visible records of their success wherever they have permanently sojourned.

Primary education of a more general and undiscriminating character, especially as to race and colour, was secured for the bulk of the West Indies by voluntary undertakings, and notably through the munificent provision of Lady Mico, which extended to the whole of the principal islands.

Thanks to Lord Harris for introducing, and to Sir Arthur Gordon for extending to the secondary stage, the public education of Trinidad, there has been since Emancipation, that is, during the last thirty-seven years, a more effective bringing together in public schools of various grades, of children of all races and ranks. Rivals at home, at school and college, in books as well as on the playground, they have very frequently gone abroad together to learn the professions they have selected.   In this way there is an intercommunion between all the

intelligent sections of the inhabitants, based
on a common training and the subtle sympathies usually generated in enlightened breasts
by intimate personal knowledge. In mixed
communities thus circumstanced, there is no
possibility of maintaining distinctions based on
mere colour, as advocated by Mr. Froude.

The following brief summary by the Rev. P.
H. Doughlin, Rector of St. Clement's, Trinidad,
a brilliant star among the sons of Ham, embodies
this fact in language which, so far as it goes,
is as comprehensive as it is weighty :—

"Who could, without seeming to insult the
intelligence of men, have predicted on the day
of Emancipation that the Negroes then re-
leased from the blight and withering influence
of ten generations of cruel bondage, so weakened and half-destroyed—so denationalized and
demoralized—so despoiled and naked, would be
in the position they are now? In spite of the
proud, supercilious, and dictatorial bearing of
their teachers, in spite of the hampering of un-
sympethetic, alien oversight, in spite of the spirit
of dependence and servility engendered by
slavery, not only have individual members of
the race entered into all the offices of dignity in

Church and State, as subalterns—as hewers of
wood and drawers of water—but they have attained to the very highest places.   Here in the
West Indies, and on the West Coast of Africa,
are to be found Surgeons of the Negro Race,
Solicitors, Barristers, Mayors, Councillors, Prin-
cipals and Founders of High Schools and Col-
leges, Editors and Proprietors of Newspapers,
Archdeacons, Bishops, Judges, and Authors
—men who not only teach those immediately around them, but also teach the world.
Members of the race have even been entrusted
with the administration of Governments.   And
it is not mere commonplace men that the Negro
Race has produced.   Not only have the British
Universities thought them worthy of their
honorary degrees and conferred them on them,
but members of the race have won these Uni-
versity degrees.   A few years back a full-blooded
Negro took the highest degree Oxford has to
give to a young man.   The European world is
looking with wonder and admiration at the
progress made by the Negro Race—a progress
unparalleled in the annals of the history of
any race."

To this we may add that in the domain

of high literature the Blacks of the United States, for the twenty-five years of social emancipation, and despite the lingering obstructions of caste prejudice, have positively achieved wonders. Leaving aside the writings of men of such high calibre as F. Douglass, Dr. Hyland Garnet, Prof. Crummell, Prof. E. Blyden, Dr. Tanner, and others, it is gratifying to be able to chronicle the Ethiopic women of North America as moving shoulder to shoulder with the men in the highest spheres of literary activity. Among a brilliant band of these our sisters, conspicuous no less in poetry than in prose, we single out but a solitary name for the double purpose of preserving brevity and of giving in one embodiment the ideal Afro-American woman of letters. The allusion here can scarcely fail to point to Mrs. S. Harper. This lady's philosophical subtlety of reasoning on grave questions finds effective expression in a prose of singular precision and vigour. But it is as a poet that posterity will hail her in the coming ages of our Race. For pathos, depth of spiritual insight, and magical exercise of a rare power of self-utterance, it will hardly be questioned that she has surpassed every com-

petitor among females—white or black—save
and except Elizabeth Barrett Browning, with
whom the gifted African stands on much the
same plane of poetic excellence.

The above summary of our past vicissitudes
and actual position shows that there is nothing
in our political circumstances to occasion uneasiness. The miserable skin and race doctrine we have been discussing does not at all
prefigure the destinies at all events of the
West Indies, or determine the motives that
will affect them. With the exception of those
belonging to the Southern States of the Union,
the vast body of African descendants now
dispersed in various countries of the Western
Hemisphere are at sufficient peace to begin
occupying themselves, according to some fixed
programme, about matters of racial importance.
More than ten millions of Africans are scattered
over the wide area indicated, and possess
amongst them instances of mental and other
qualifications which render them remarkable
among their fellow-men. But like the essential
parts of a complicated albeit perfect machine,
these attainments and qualifications so widely
dispersed await, it is evident, some potential

agency to collect and adjust them into the vast engine essential for executing the true purposes of the civilized African Race. Already, especially since the late Emancipation Jubilee, are signs manifest of a desire for intercommunion and intercomprehension amongst the more distinguished of our people. With intercourse and unity of purpose will be secured the means to carry out the obvious duties which are sure to devolve upon us, especially with reference to the cradle of our Race, which is most probably destined to be the ultimate resting-place and headquarters of millions of our posterity. Within the short time that we had to compass all that we have achieved, there could not have arisen opportunities for doing more than we have effected. Meanwhile our present device is : " Work, Hope, and Wait! ".

Finally, it must be borne in mind that the abolition of physical bondage did not by any means secure all the requisite conditions of "a fair field and no favour" for the future career of the freedmen. The remnant of Jacob, on their return from the Captivity, were compelled, whilst rebuilding their Temple, literally to labour with the working tool in one hand

and the sword for personal defence in the other.
Even so have the conditions, figuratively,
presented themselves under which the Blacks
have been obliged to rear the fabric of self-
elevation since 1838, whilst combating cease-
lessly the obstacles opposed to the realizing
of their legitimate aspirations. Mental and,
in many cases, material success has been gained,
but the machinery for accumulating and applying the means required for comprehensive
racial enterprises is waiting on Providence,
time, and circumstances for its establishment
and successful working.

UNWIN BROTHERS, THE GRESHAM PRESS, CHILWORTH AND LONDON.